P9-DTX-630

SHAKESPEARE
AND THE BAWDY COURT
OF STRATFORD

Some other works of Dr. Brinkworth:

'The Study and Use of Archdeacons' Court Records', *Transactions of the Royal Historical Society* (1942)

The Archdeacon's Court, Liber Actorum, 1584, 2 vols. (Oxfordshire Record Society)

Episcopal Visitation Book for the Archdeaconry of Buckingham, 1662 (Buckinghamshire Record Society)

South Newington Churchwardens' Accounts, 1553-1684 (Banbury Historical Society)

Old Banbury (Banbury Historical Society)

SHAKESPEARE

and the

BAWDY COURT

of

STRATFORD

E.R.C. BRINKWORTH

Illustrated by **Wendy Jones**

PHILLIMORE
London and Chichester

1972

Published by
PHILLIMORE & CO. LTD.
Shopwyke Hall, Chichester, Sussex, England.

SBN 900592 82 6

Text set by Phillimore in 11 pt. Press Roman
Printed in Great Britain by Fletcher & Son Ltd., Norwich.

CONTENTS

ILLUSTRATIONS

ACKNOWLEDGMENTS

THE HISTORICAL RECORDS upon which this book is based are among the Sackville of Knole Manuscripts deposited in the Kent Archives Office, and I have to thank the owner, Lord Sackville, for most kindly giving me permission to use them. My thanks are also due to the County Archivist, Dr. Felix Hull, for ready help upon many occasions. It was Mr. Hugh Hanley, now of the Buckinghamshire Record Office, who, in an article in the *Times Literary Supplement* for 21 May, 1964, first drew my attention to the existence of the Stratford Peculiar Court records in the Sackville MSS., and led me to the full investigation of them which has resulted in the present volume. The unique drawing of Shakespeare's home, New Place, demolished in 1702, is among the Portland Papers in the British Museum, and it is reproduced here by kind permission of His Grace the Duke of Portland.

I owe a large debt of gratitude to Mr. Philip Styles, Reader in English History in the University of Birmingham, for advice; I would like to thank Mr. E.T. Lean for valuable facts and suggestions; also Dr. D.M. Barratt, of the Bodleian Library, and Miss M. Henderson, of the Worcestershire Record Office, who have read the manuscript. To Jeremy Gibson, who has given me constant encouragement and help from the start, and to my wife, who has assisted me throughout, I am also grateful.

Faults and flaws are entirely my responsibility.

E.R.C.B.

PART I

THE 'BAWDY COURTS'
AND NEW LIGHT ON SHAKESPEARE

THE STRATFORD BACKGROUND

THE 'BAWDY COURTS'
AND NEW LIGHT ON SHAKESPEARE

THE STRATFORD BACKGROUND

THERE IS ONE important — and fascinating — aspect of Shakespeare's life and of Shakespeare's Stratford which is still unknown. It seems incredible. How can this be, after all the work that has been done, all the books that have been written upon these subjects? The astonishing answer is that the secrets lie hidden in certain historical records which until now have remained almost wholly unexplored. They are the records of the Church Court, or 'Bawdy Court' as it was generally called, held regularly at Stratford-upon-Avon during Shakespeare's lifetime.

To modern minds this must appear a most unlikely source, for Church Courts mean next to nothing today. But in Shakespeare's time they were an ever-present reality and loomed large in the everyday life of every man and woman in the land. Everyone was subject to the Church Courts because everyone was by law as much a member of the Church as of the State. And the church courts covered not only church affairs but a great area of the whole of life, including its most intimate parts. As Professor A.G. Dickens vividly puts it, the courts 'ground through their ancient routines, keeping the morals of all men under observation; their notaries scribbled down the sins and quarrels of society in spidery hands across those countless pages with which modern historians are only now gradually becoming more familiar'.[1]

One of our foremost historians, Professor G.R. Elton, has recently summed up the situation. After remarking on the scant attention which church court records generally have received from historians, saying indeed that they have 'scarcely

3

THE SHAKESPEARE FAMILY

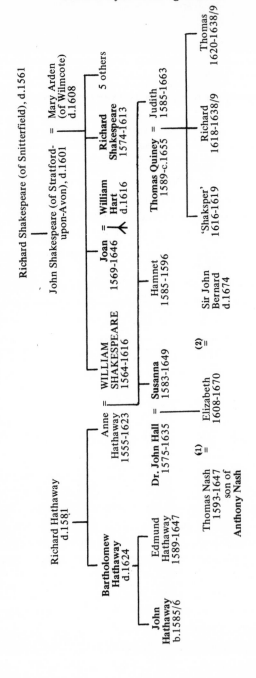

Persons mentioned in the Act Books shown in bold type

been touched', he goes on to emphasise their potentialities: they 'offer a most promising field to research because they illuminate the history of church and people in ways which no other source can. They take one to the realities. This is because of the wide range of cases which came before these courts and because that range touched the human being so very near his personal centre . . . The information available on this wide range of issues . . . would add great detail, precision and depth to our knowledge of people, both lay and spiritual, at all levels of society'.[2]

Church Courts were held in their hundreds regularly all over the country. Each of the two archbishops, every bishop and every archdeacon had a court. In addition there were some 300 independent or semi-independent 'peculiar' jurisdictions, each with its court. The parish of Stratford-upon-Avon was one of these peculiars. It comprised the Borough, the chapelries of Luddington and Bishopton, with Bridgetown, Clopton, Dodwell, Drayton, Ruin Clifton, Shottery and Welcombe. For two years out of every three it was independent of the Bishop of Worcester in whose diocese it then lay. The Stratford court sat in the parish church about once a month with the Vicar sitting as 'Ordinary' or Judge. The notary of the court or his deputy wrote down the proceedings in his Act Books.

Fortunately, some of these Stratford court records have been preserved. In particular there are two Act Books, one covering parts of the last 26 years of Shakespeare's life, that is, between 1590 and 1616; and the other covering the years 1622 and 1624, that is, the six to eight years after his death, when conditions had altered but little. No other Stratford records exist which reveal the times in anything like such depth and detail; or anything like so vividly. In this book they are studied for the first time.

In these records we meet several people nearest to Shakespeare: his elder daughter Susanna, his son-in-law Thomas Quiney, husband of his other daughter Judith, his brother Richard, his sister Joan and his brother-in-law Bartholomew Hathaway.

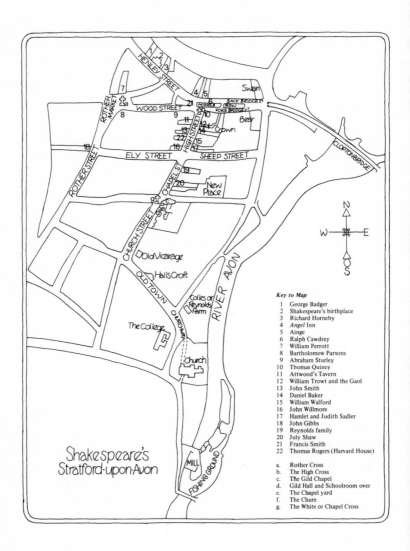

Shakespeare's
Stratford-upon-Avon

Key to Map

1 George Badger
2 Shakespeare's birthplace
3 Richard Horneby
4 *Angel* Inn
5 Ainge
6 Ralph Cawdrey
7 William Perrott
8 Bartholomew Parsons
9 Abraham Sturley
10 Thomas Quiney
11 Attwood's Tavern
12 William Trowt and the Gaol
13 John Smith
14 Daniel Baker
15 William Walford
16 John Willmore
17 Hamlet and Judith Sadler
18 John Gibbs
19 Reynolds family
20 July Shaw
21 Francis Smith
22 Thomas Rogers (Harvard House)

a. Rother Cross
b. The High Cross
c. The Gild Chapel
d. Gild Hall and Schoolroom over
e. The Chapel yard
f. The Chure
g. The White or Chapel Cross

We meet also some of Shakespeare's intimate friends and many contemporaries who must have been familiar to him. Fascinating and hitherto unknown details of their lives are forthcoming. As Professor C.J. Sisson says, 'Whatever adds to our knowledge of the world of men in which he (Shakespeare) had personal contacts has an especial interest for us'.[3]

Much new light is shed on the making of Shakespeare's will and upon the circumstances of his death − light which makes necessary a re-appraisal of traditions which have long held the field.

New light is shed, too, upon the religion of Shakespeare's daughter Susanna and through her, upon that of the poet himself.

But what is even more important, these Act Books show how intimately and continuously the life of Shakespeare, in common with that of everyman, was affected by the church courts: how much these courts were part and parcel of his mind and experience. They present a new aspect of Shakespeare's life, Shakespeare's Stratford and Shakespeare's England.

Reading these court records of Stratford, the whole place comes alive as it was in Shakespeare's day. The people we find in them are the people who lived out their lives there. The lay-out of the place has altered so little that very often we can identify the very houses they occupied. Map in hand we can re-live the past.

The town or borough of Stratford had about 2,000 inhabitants. There were about 217 houses, some of them the fine timbered buildings we see today, though these for the most part date only from the rebuilding after the three great fires which ravaged the town during Shakespeare's lifetime.

It was a tree-embowered place; there were a thousand elms as well as other trees. Farming was at the doors, country sights and sounds and smells were everywhere. But it was certainly no rural retreat: it was agog with business, especially on market days and at fair times. There were upwards of a dozen trade companies. The High Cross stood at the top of Bridge Street, a wooden structure on four pillars with a clock turret on top. Opposite this was the Cage, at one time a prison; a little further along High Street was the Gaol; at the southern end of High Street stood the pillory and possibly also the whipping post and the stocks and the ducking-stool. There were crosses at other busy centres, the White or Chapel Cross by the Gild Chapel and the Cross in the Rother Market. There were four inns in Bridge Street, then the busiest area in the town — the *Swan*, the *Bear*, the *Crown* and the *Angel*. About the town were numbers of taverns and alehouses. The Chapel, Gild Hall, Grammar School and Almshouse formed a serene central group. The second largest private residence was New Place, 'a pretty house of brick and timber' as Leland described it, the home of Shakespeare, previously owned by the magnate Sir Hugh Clopton, builder of the great bridge over the Avon by which Stratford is approached from the east.

Around the town lay the hamlets, making up the rest of the parish and bringing the population to 3,000: Bishopton and Luddington, each with a chapel, Bridgetown, Clopton, Dodwell, Drayton, Ruin Clifton, Shottery and Welcombe.

The great parish church stood, as now, apart from the town, out in Old Stratford, on the banks of the Avon.

The location of the court within the church is uncertain, but judging from other places, it was perhaps at the west end of the north aisle, between the porch and the west wall, though most likely it was held in the room over the porch which down the centuries has served as an *officium*. It would be fitted up rather like the court in Chester Cathedral, the only one still preserved as it was when in action: a raised seat for the Judge (the Vicar) and below that a large table for the notary, who sat at the head of it, and the witnesses who sat round it. The crier of the court stood near the notary and the accused stood facing the Judge. The hours were usually from 8 to 12 with, sometimes, sittings also in the afternoon. The court sat at about monthly intervals, with a longer recess at harvest time. Occasional hearings were held in the house of the Judge, the Vicarage.

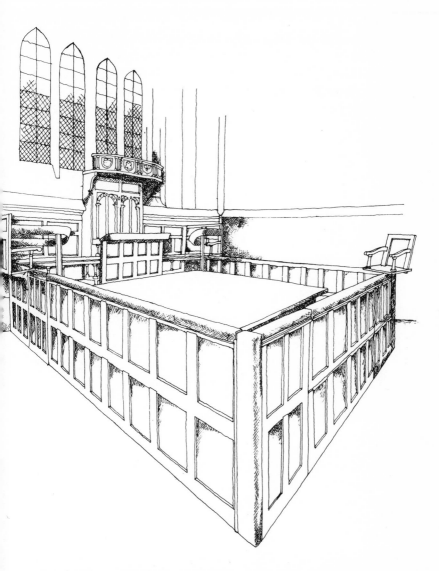

Fig. 1. THE CONSISTORY COURT IN CHESTER CATHEDRAL
This is the only church court still preserved as it was when in action.
The raised throne was for the Judge (at Stratford the Vicar).
The Notary sat at the head of the table, the witnesses around it,
and the accused stood facing the Judge.

This, then, was the court as it would be familiar to Shakespeare and his fellow Stratfordians, the centre of such an important part of their lives; the place which saw the re-enactment of innumerable comedies and tragedies of everyday local life.

REFERENCES

1 A.G. Dickens, *The English Reformation* (1964), p.69.

2 G.R. Elton, *England, 1200-1640: The Sources of History* (1969), pp.105-6.

3 'Shakespeare's Friends: Hathaways and Burmans of Shottery' in *Shakespeare Survey*, no. 12 (1959), p.95.

PART II

THE STRATFORD CHURCH COURT

HOW THE CHURCH COURTS WORKED

IT IS NOW NECESSARY to describe briefly how the court worked, the main outlines of court procedure: not, perhaps, the most thrilling of subjects, but worth while for the sake of following the records: and, of course, the procedure itself took a very important part in the life of the time. It is an aspect of social and religious history that has been all too little regarded and is well worth attention for its own sake.[1]

We begin with the annual or occasionally bi-annual Visitation or inspection, held by the Vicar as head of the jurisdiction. Apart from the court officials, the key figures were the churchwardens, for upon them devolved the all-important duty of making a report upon the parish; not a mere general report: names had to be named. To guide them in this arduous task the wardens were given when they were sworn in upon taking office a list of 'Articles of Inquiry' so that they knew what to look out for. A long list it certainly was and in many particulars it went very near the bone. Who was guilty of 'adultery, whoredom, incest, drunkenness, swearing, ribaldry, usury' and any other 'uncleanness and wickedness of life'? Who was guilty of absence from church on Sundays and holy days or from Holy Communion at Easter, of rude and disorderly behaviour in church, of brawling in church (or in the court), of breaking the Sabbath and holy days, of blasphemy, of scandalmongering, of not contributing to the church rate, of bigamy or irregular marriage, of not proving wills or taking out administrations? Was the church in good repair and was it provided with the necessary books and goods and were these in a respectable condition? Were all schoolmasters, physicians, surgeons and midwives duly licensed by the church authorities?

13

These were the main questions asked — there were many others — and it was no doubt with much anxiety and heart-searching that the wardens compiled their answers, or in technical language, made up their 'Bill of Detection' in which they reported or 'presented' the transgressors. For the most part they relied on proved fact, but they could report a person merely on the strength of rumour. Information reached the court not only from these official presentments but also from the reports of its apparitors and from other sources. The Judge could proceed upon these by virtue of his office alone.

The reports having reached the court, they were examined and sifted and a list drawn up of persons who were to be called to answer a charge. The notary or his clerk wrote out a summons (or 'citation') against each of these persons ordering appearance before the court on a given day.

These citations were delivered by the messenger of the court (the 'apparitor') upon the person of the accused. In practice, citation was often by word of mouth alone; or by the showing of what was called an 'English note' which stated the gist of the matter. The apparitor was a well-known figure locally and his calls were pretty sure to be seen and gossiped about. Sometimes he failed to make a personal delivery because the accused hid himself or resorted to some other subterfuge. The Judge then ordered a further citation to be made 'by ways and means', as the phrase went, such as by fixing the citation on the door of the house of the accused or on the door of the parish church. Citations were also read out regularly from the pulpit of the parish church just before the sermon on Sundays. Here was more material for gossip as the people wandered back up the long Church Way after service.

When the accused appeared in court the charge was named (or 'objected') to him, he then took the oath and then either admitted the charge or denied it. If he admitted it the Judge either dismissed him, usually with a warning ('monition') not to offend in the like manner again; or ordered him to do penance, which meant open confession of the offence. This was a heavy penalty, and for most people a dreaded one. It was an age in which a person's credit and reputation were regarded as of the utmost importance; the humiliation of a public penance was so much the greater punishment the higher up the social scale the person was.[2]

Penance was either fully public, in the parish church before the whole congregation in service time, usually Morning Prayer; or semi-public, before the minister and officials (sometimes the secular officials of the town were included) in church or in the relative seclusion of the chapel at Bishopton or in some other 'convenient place'.

The aim of the Judge in ordering penance was to make the punishment fit the crime. A fully public penance was conducted by the minister standing in the pulpit. The penitent was required to confess the sin in intimate detail, standing on a stool in the middle aisle near the pulpit, clad either in ordinary clothes or, for the most serious offences, enveloped in a white sheet, bareheaded, barefooted, and holding a white rod. The length of time varied too: some had to stand for the whole length of the service, some until the end of the sermon, some only until the end of the second lesson.[3] Some had to do penance on more than one Sunday; some in the Gild Chapel as well as the church. Some in addition had to suffer the shame of a white sheet penance in the Market Place. Thursday is often mentioned. It was then the weekly Market Day.

Penance was a frequent occurrence and must have provided a welcome diversion in the two-hours' tedium of a Sunday morning service; a washing of dirty linen indeed, a savoury substitute for the Sunday papers of today.

An offender was sometimes allowed to commute the whole or part of penance into a money payment. The Judge fixed the amount and specified the purpose to which the money was to be applied. The poor of the parish appear to have had the first claim at Stratford. The amounts were, relatively to certain other places, small. There are several instances of what may be called implied commutations, where no penance is specifically mentioned, but merely the sum to be paid, usually 12 pence.

When the accused had made satisfaction either by the performance of penance or by the payment of commutation money and had settled the fees, he was dismissed.

If the accused denied the charge, the Judge ordered him to 'purge' himself, either on his own oath alone, swearing his innocence, or on his own oath backed by a specified number of his neighbours, called his 'compurgators'. A proclamation giving notice that the purgation was to be made on such a day had to be given out in the parish church at least six days before. It called on all who had grounds for opposing the purgation and/or the compurgators to appear on a specified court day and bring forward their objections. A further proclamation had to be made on the court day three times in a loud voice for opposers to appear. If objections at either stage were proved, or if the accused failed to produce compurgators, he was reckoned guilty and ordered to perform penance.

If the accused did not obey the summons ('citation') and appear in court on the specified day he was called three times in a loud voice and then formally pronounced to be disobedient ('contumacious'). By this he incurred excommunication. The Judge either pronounced the sentence there and then or reserved it to a specified sitting, very often to the next court day. In technical terms he 'continued the certificate' or deferred the proof of service of the citation.

Excommunication was the penalty for contumacy (or disobedience) of all kinds, including failure to obey an order to carry out duties, to provide required church goods, to effect repairs, etc.

The execution of all orders, from the original citation onwards, had to be certified, either by word of mouth or in writing. The function of Church Courts was therefore administrative as well as judicial.

Excommunication was of two kinds, minor and major. The minor excommunication excluded the offender from the services and sacraments of the church. This is what the sentence implied in the first instance. If the accused persisted in his disobedience he incurred the major excommunication. This added the further penalty of exclusion from society ('the communion of the faithful'); and it could have grave secular consequences for it largely cut him off from commerce and the protection of the law.

The list of those excommunicated (in the 'schedule of excommunication') was read out, along with citations, before the sermon on Sunday mornings.

If after 40 days a person still remained excommunicated the offence was said to be 'aggravated' and he was liable by law to be handed over to the secular authorities for imprisonment. This was a costly procedure. There are no examples of it in the present records.

In theory, and occasionally in practice, anyone who had anything to do with an excommunicate thereby came under the sentence himself also.

Excommunication was also incurred *ipso facto* for certain offences, e.g. for 'brawling' in church or churchyard.[4]

The ban of excommunication could only be lifted by formal Absolution. To obtain this the culprit had humbly to petition the Judge and take the oath 'to obey the law and stand by the commandments of the church'. Then, having carried out the requirements of the court and any orders and obligations pending, he was absolved and dismissed.

Fees were demanded by the court at every turn. They are not often mentioned in the present records, but such as are entered show that they correspond fairly closely to the tariff set forth in Archbishop Whitgift's Table of Fees of 1597. Bearing in mind the relative value of money then it will be seen how heavy a burden these fees were. The most common were as follows:

	Judge	*Registrar*
Citations	5d.	5d.
Exhibiting Bill of Detection ... ... (by churchwardens)		4d.
Production of first witness	9d.	4d.
Production of every other witness ...	4½d.	4½d.
Purgation	9d.	9d.
Excommunication	8d.	8d.
Absolution	9d.	9d.
Certificate of Absolution	8d.	8d.

To the apparitor for the execution of any process: 2d. per mile. At Stratford many of the apparitor's visits would take him far less than a mile. It would be interesting to know whether he got the full 2d. or only a fraction of it.

Contentious cases, i.e., those which were the equivalent of civil cases in the secular courts, were technically called 'instance' cases. Normally in the Church Courts these were dealt with in separate sessions and involved a much more complicated procedure. At Stratford, being but a small jurisdiction, it seems that the summary procedure of ordinary 'office' cases was regarded as sufficient.

Paupers were excused fees and no doubt there were concessions such as Dr. Marchant notes in the Norwich Consistory Court where many defendants did not answer to their first citation and were excommunicated, but the sentence was regarded as a technical one and only 3d. or 6d. was demanded for absolution.[5]

The procedure in testamentary cases may be briefly outlined. Most of these in the present records are to do with the proving of wills in common form and the granting of administration.

The executor merely presented the will to the Judge and in the absence and without the calling of such as had interest, produced witnesses to prove the will. The witnesses testified upon their oaths that the will exhibited was the true, whole and last testament of the deceased, and further swore to make true answer to such questions as the Judge demanded of them concerning the will. The Judge thereupon (and sometimes upon lesser proof) annexed his probate and seal to the will, whereby it was confirmed. The executor swore that he believed it to be the last will and testament of the deceased; that he would pay all debts and legacies so far as the goods extended; that he would cause the goods to be apprized and make or cause to be made a true and perfect inventory by a day appointed by the Judge if none were exhibited at the time; that he would make or cause to be made a true and just account of the goods when he should be lawfully called to do so.[6]

The Law which the Courts Administered

The pre-Reformation canon law still remained in force in so far as it was not repugnant to the royal prerogative and the rights and customs of the kingdom.[7]

For the day-to-day working of the courts such as the one at Stratford, all the Judge needed to know was the Rubrics of the Book of Common Prayer, the Elizabethan Injunctions of 1559 as interpreted by Injunctions of the local Ordinary, i.e. at Stratford, the Judge, the Vicar, a few Acts of Parliament (especially 5-6 Edward VI, which declared certain persons excommunicate *ipso facto*), the Canons of 1597, and, after 1603, the Canons of that year.[8]

REFERENCES

1 This is only an outline of the main lines of procedure as far as the present records are concerned. See for fuller treatment and the forms, Thomas Oughton, *Ordo Judiciorum*, 2 vols. (1728-38). A good short account is in Henry Conset, *The Practice of the Spiritual Courts* (2nd ed., 1700), especially pp.379-396 on summary procedure.

2 R.A. Marchant, *The Church under the Law* (1969), p.178.

3 The following is a key to the various points in the service at which
   Penance was ordered:
   Morning Prayer consisted of Mattins (with the 1st and 2nd
   Lessons); the Litany; Altar Prayers, the course of which was, the
   Lord's Prayer, the Collect, the Ten Commandments, the Prayer
   for the Monarch, the Epistle, the Gospel, the Creed, the reading
   of notices, Briefs, Citations and Excommunications, the Sermon
   or reading of one of the Homilies, the Offertory, the Prayer for
   the Church Militant.

   See G.W.O. Addleshaw and F. Etchells, *The Architectural Setting of
   Anglican Worship* (1948), pp.70-71.

4 5-6 Edward VI cap. 6, sect. 2.

5 R.A. Marchant, *op. cit.*, pp.19, 204 n.

6 The best and fullest modern account is in E.F. Jacob (ed.) *The
   Register of Henry Chichele* (Cant. and York Soc.), vol. 2, Introduction.

7 By 25 Henry VIII, c.19 (1533).

8 R.A. Marchant, *op. cit.*, the section 'Disciplinary Law', pp.128-134.
   For the general principles of the law, see R.C. Mortimer, *Western
   Canon Law* (1953), especially Chapter 4, 'The Canon Law in England
   after the Reformation'; and E. Garth Moore, *An Introduction to
   English Canon Law* (1967).

JUDGES AND OFFICIALS OF THE COURT

Vicars

The Vicar of the parish of Stratford-upon-Avon was the Judge of the Peculiar Court.

John Bramhall was Vicar from 1589 to 1596. In his time the Vicarage was in Church Street, on the east side near the turn into Old Town. Bramhall was a thorough-going Puritan and Sabbatarian. He declared that the great fires which ravaged Stratford in 1594 and 1595 were sent in retribution for the prevalent desecration of the Sabbath.[1]

Richard Byfield, Vicar from 1596 to 1605, was like Bramhall a strong Puritan. His two sons Nicholas and Richard were prominent figures in the Sabbatarian controversy. (See further under **Abuse of Sunday and Holy-Days**, page 51.)

John Rogers, Vicar from 1605 to 1619, did not live in the Vicarage near the church. After one or two moves the Corporation in 1611 settled him in the old Priests' house in Chapel Quad, next to the schoolmaster, Alexander Aspinall. Thus he became a near neighbour of Shakespeare at New Place, over the road. He officiated at the funeral of Shakespeare on 25 April 1616.

Thomas Wilson, Vicar from 1619 to 1638, also lived in Chapel Quad. Like his immediate predecessors he was an advanced Puritan. He got into trouble with the higher authorities for particularizing against certain individuals in his sermons, for not wearing the surplice, for not insisting on kneeling for the reception of the Holy Communion, for not using the sign of the cross in baptism and the ring in marriage. There was much religious strife in Stratford during his régime.[2] One of his strong supporters, Dr. John Hall, son-in-law of Shakespeare, appears in our records; so does a leader of the opposition, John Lane of the Alveston manor family.

Notaries Public

The acts of the court had to be done in the presence of a notary public. In theory, and sometimes in fact, he wrote the acts, though often a clerk under him performed this office. Some of the notaries probably worked in more than one court, including the Bishop's Court at Worcester.

Of the notaries a few details are forthcoming about Richard Lewes *alias* Williams whose name occurs in the headings to sessions from 13 April to 2 December 1608. He was probably the son of Thomas Lewes ap Williams who became Bailiff in 1564, one of the few Welshmen to rise to high office in Stratford, though there were many in the town, evidence of the fact that it was on one of the main cattle-droving routes from Wales to London.[3] Some 20 people bearing Welsh surnames occur in these two court Act Books.

Apparitors

The apparitors in a small jurisdiction like Stratford were probably part-time men doing other jobs as well. Though Greene was one of the commonest names in Stratford, the Richard Greene who appears as apparitor in all the surviving court records between February 1606/7 and 26 March 1616 may perhaps be identified with the Richard Greene who in the Parish Register record of his burial on 20 August 1617 is described as parish clerk.

It is likely that at Stratford the apparitor acted also as crier of the court.

Churchwardens

These officials, upon whom the administration of church and parish so much depended, were chosen from 'the better sort', the more substantial men of the parish and the borough.

Their chief duties, as far as we are concerned, were

1.　　to 'present' or report all offenders to the court;

2.　　to certify the performance of court orders;

3.   to see that the church and church property were in good repair;
4.   to see that the books and articles required were provided and kept in good condition;
5.   to see that all attended church at the required times and behaved themselves there.

Among the Stratford churchwardens who appear in these records as taking their oaths at Visitations are three particularly close to Shakespeare.

Bartholomew Hathaway, sworn on 13 April 1608, was Shakespeare's brother-in-law; John Hathaway, sworn on 24 May 1622, was a nephew, son of Bartholomew.[4] John followed his father in the office and first took his oath at Eastertide 1616, only a few days before the death of his uncle, William Shakespeare. He would attend the funeral service and the burial in the chancel on 25 April both in his official capacity and as a chief family mourner. John Hathaway was the executor of his father and appeared in court on 6 December 1624 to prove the will (see under the heading **Wills and Bequests**, page 106).

'July' or Julian Shaw, sworn on 25 November 1620, was the son of Ralph Shaw, wool merchant, a friend and neighbour in Henley Street of John Shakespeare, William's father. July himself, maltster and wool merchant, became alderman and bailiff. He in turn was a close friend of William Shakespeare. He was one of the four witnesses to Shakespeare's will. He lived in Chapel Street; the house has a plaque bearing his name.

Two other wardens should be especially mentioned. John Willmore (or Woolmer) took his oath along with Bartholomew Hathaway in 1608. He lived in the fine house in High Street at the corner of Ely Street. Next but one to it stands the house with the finest carved front in Stratford. It belonged to Alderman Thomas Rogers whose daughter Willmore married. Another of Alderman Rogers' daughters married Robert Harvard. Their son, John, founded Harvard University, and it is thus the Rogers' home in High Street has come to be called Harvard House.

Stephen Burman, of the substantial Shottery family, took his oath as churchwarden on 24 May 1622. He is ranked as 'gentleman'.

Richard Tyler was called as warden to the Visitation of 3 May 1625. He had been a sidesman in 1622. It was during his years of office that the repairs to the chancel of the parish church, where Shakespeare lay buried, were at last, after a half-century of gross neglect, completed and other parts of the church put into decent order. Tyler was the son of William Tyler who had been a colleague of the poet's father John Shakespeare as constable.

Sidesmen

Turning to the sidesmen,[5] there are several who should be noted particularly. The entries in the court acts about them bring some of their activities before us in welcome detail.

On 9 November 1590 the four sidesmen, John Barber, Avery[6] Edwards, Richard Horneby and Nicholas Tibbotts were called to answer for the lack of certain required books in the parish church. Horneby and Tibbotts were bound (although Tibbotts in fact was absent) that henceforth on each Sunday and festival day 'the said Horneby with his fellow churchwarden[7] assisted with the constable or some other in Stratford . . . shall each Sabbath day and festival day in time of divine service or sermon go through the parish of Stratford aforesaid and view and see what manner of persons are in any alehouses or inns or other suspected places . . . gaming or tippling or otherwise and to present the names as well of the householders as of the offenders at the next court'. And Barber and Edwards were bound 'that they do diligently view and see what persons do use to bowl or play at any other games at any times aforesaid and to present the same'.

John Barber was the brother of Thomas Barber, three times bailiff and for many years host of the *Bear*, the well set up inn at the bottom of Fore Bridge Street. Both his first and his second wife were avowed Catholics and he himself may be presumed to be at least a sympathiser. Certainly he was no

Fig. 2. HARVARD HOUSE, HIGH STREET
This house belonged to Alderman Thomas Rogers. His daughter
married John Willmore (or Woolmer) who took his oath as churchwarden
at the Visitation in 1608.

Puritan and he gave a warm welcome to the companies of players who frequently performed before the public in his yard.[8]

We find in our records a son of Thomas Barber, also named Thomas, called to the court as churchwarden of Luddington in May 1622.

Richard Horneby was a man Shakespeare knew intimately from his earliest days. He kept the blacksmith's shop in Henley Street just to the west of the Mere stream as it crossed the road and flowed by way of Rother Street and Chapel Lane to the river.[9]

Nicholas Tibbotts was a brother of Thomas Tibbotts, the attorney who negotiated in 1602 the transfer of a cottage opposite New Place from Walter Getley to William Shakespeare. It has been conjectured that Shakespeare wanted it for a servant.

The sidesmen William Wylitt and John Smith were called on 10 October 1592 because they had omitted to levy the 12-penny fine 'according to the statute'[10] on those who did not attend church. They were ordered to collect it and to certify on each court day that they had done so. Insistence on the collection of this levy is found elsewhere in our records.

At the same court on 10 October the sidesmen for the preceding year, Abraham Sturley and Arthur Boys, had to answer for detaining the small sum of 12 pence bequeathed to the parish in the will of one Arthur Newell. There is no entry as to the outcome: but the mere fact of the charge is an indication of the court's attention to detail.

Sturley was bailiff in 1596. He was a brother-in-law of Richard Quiney, Shakespeare's great friend. He lived in a fine house which he had built after the great fire of 1594. It now has a brick front. An original plaster ceiling graces a room on the ground floor.

An echo of Sturley occurs in a court hearing early in May 1606. Thomas Hiccox (good Stratford name) had apparently been in dispute with a neighbour. He gained dismissal 'inasmuch as Master Abraham Sturley testified that they agree'.

One of the sidesmen sworn at the Visitation of 13 April 1608 was William Walford. He was a rich woollen draper. After the fire of 1595 he built a house on the east side of High Street, one of those in Stratford which have been restored to present something like the original appearance.

Curates

Among the curates found in the court records are three about whom further interesting details are available.[11]

William Gilbert *alias* Higges was curate of Stratford for many years. He appears acting as notary in all the surviving court records between 1600 and December 1606; and as exhibiting his licence at the Visitation of 1608. It has been suggested that he was the original of Sir Nathaniel in *Love's Labour's Lost*: 'a foolish, mild man, an honest man, look you, and soon dashed; he is a marvellous good neighbour, faith, and a very good bowler'.[12] Gilbert lived in quarters in the Gild precinct over the way from Shakespeare's house, New Place. To augment his meagre stipend as curate, Gilbert did a variety of jobs. He minded the clock of the High Cross house; he drew up wills; he assisted at the Grammar School; and here we find him picking up the odd fee or two as a deputy notary of the local church court.

John Marshall was for many years curate of the chapelry of Bishopton in the parish of Stratford. On one occasion, 25 November 1602, we find him acting with William Gilbert as deputy for the notary public. Marshall was a Master of Arts of St. Alban Hall, Oxford. His library, listed in detail after his death by Abraham Sturley (whom we have met before), shows both the extent of his learning — beyond that of most clerics of his day — and its strong Puritan bias. He had Latin, Greek and Hebrew grammars and dictionaries, a good selection of the Latin classics, numerous commentaries on Scripture, Calvin's *Institutes*, a useful range of Protestant sermons, books of devotion, Ascham's *Schoolmaster*, Clifford's *Witches*; and a book on fishing.

George Quiney was the son of Richard Quiney, Shakespeare's close friend who became Bailiff in 1602 and was
killed during his year of office in trying to stop a brawl. George
Quiney graduated from Balliol College, Oxford, took holy
orders and became curate of his native place. We find him
presenting his letters of orders at the Visitation of May 1622.
He occurs also several times, reading out citations and other
court documents in the parish church and conducting penances
there. He assisted with the teaching in the Grammar School.
He fell ill — it seems of tuberculosis — and was attended by
Dr. John Hall. He died in April 1624 at the age of 24. Hall
wrote of him in his case-book: 'Many things having been tried
to no purpose, peacefully he fell asleep in the Lord. He was
of good understanding, skilled in languages and for a young
man widely learned'.[13]

REFERENCES

1   E.I. Fripp, *Shakespeare's Stratford*, p.55.

2   P. Styles, 'The Borough of Stratford-upon-Avon' in *The Victoria
     History of the County of Warwick*, vol. 3 (1945), p.281.

3   *Ibid.,* p.236.

4   See C.J. Sisson, 'Shakespeare's Friends: Hathaways and Burmans
     of Shottery', *Shakespeare Survey* no. 12 (1959).

5   The word in the original is *economi*; churchwardens are called
     gardiani. In *The Revised Medieval Latin Word List*, prepared by
     R.E. Latham (1965), *economus* in the ecclesiastical sense is given
     as meaning 'churchwarden', but at Stratford it evidently meant
     'sidesman'. This is the word used along with 'churchwarden'
     when entries were in English.

6   So he is called in the Parish Register. The original has *Avaricius.*

7   The word is used loosely here for 'sidesman' which Horneby
     clearly was.

8   See E.I. Fripp, *op. cit.*, pp.8-10.

9   Fripp's delightful conjecture (*ibid.*, p.16) must be quoted. He
     tells us that next to Horneby's smithy were a pair of cottages owned
     by the eccentric tailor Wedgewood and next to them, the block of
     three houses (including the Birthplace) owned by Alderman
     Shakespeare. Fripp suggests that in *King John* we have a picture
     of Wedgewood haranguing Horneby:

> I saw a smith stand with his hammer, thus,
> The whilst his iron did on the anvil cool,
> With open mouth swallowing a tailor's news;
> Who, with his shears and measures in his hand,
> Standing on slippers, — which his nimble haste
> Had falsely thrust upon contrary feet . . .

4: 2: 193-8

10   i.e. The Act of Uniformity, 1559.

11   Apart from their court activities, the information comes from
     the invaluable Fripp: for William Gilbert, see Fripp, *Shakespeare's
     Stratford*, p.51 and *Shakespeare's Haunts*, p.29; for John Marshall,
     Shakespeare's Haunts, pp.51-52; for George Quiney, *Shakespeare's
     Stratford*, p.73.

12   5: 2: 584.

13   I have altered the translation given in Fripp.

THE STRATFORD CHURCH COURT:
ITS EFFICIENCY, ITS ADMINISTRATION AND ITS RECORDS

COMPLAINTS had long been made against the church courts: of blackmail and corruption, of favouritism, of the ex-officio oath,[1] of excessive fees, commutation, excommunication;[2] indeed there were, as Archbishop Whitgift said, 'a multitude of complaints'.

Many of the complaints came to a head and received vehement expression in the reign of Elizabeth I and later. 'The bawdy court' it was everywhere called.[3] Stratford was not to be outdone. Here we have one Thomas Faux 'scandalizing this court and saying it was the bawdy court'. There are several examples in these records of obscenities shouted against the court during sittings in the parish church. Nevertheless the Church Court system was generally regarded as a necessary bulwark of good order in society.

From the evidence available it is apparent that church courts varied considerably in standards of probity and efficiency as between different places and at different times. As far as Stratford is concerned in these records there is no evidence of corruption or of excessive fees; the commutations are modest. The distinct impression is that, within the limits of the system, there was just and considerate dealing. There is ample evidence that the court was no respecter of persons, at least as far as detection and citation were concerned.

How efficient was the court? Any answer to this question must take into account that all courts, secular as well as spiritual – indeed all organs of administration – were by modern standards grossly inefficient. Here in Stratford we encounter what we today would call a pretty haphazard way of conducting business. We find people having to be cited repeatedly; people ignoring the orders of the court for months on end; people remaining long excommunicated. Nevertheless in the majority of cases the accused eventually appeared and obeyed; and the excommunicated usually sought absolution. In small jurisdictions like Stratford, where the authorities could keep an eye on every single person, no doubt few ventured to defy the sentence for long periods as they often did elsewhere. As to the number of persons affected by the court it is clear that here as elsewhere a large proportion of the adult population came, to a greater or lesser degree, within its procedure. These number, in the first Act Book, 253, and, in the second, 161.[4]

A few points may be suggested towards the interpretation of these records. The churchwardens and sidesmen, in making their presentments, were operating in a tiny world in which everyone was known intimately to everyone else; nothing could be hidden from them. They were men exercising but a brief authority: and if while in office they were exposed to verbal abuse, when out of it they might expect retaliation from those they had presented: there were many temptations to turn the blind eye and the deaf ear. But bearing in mind the checks and balances of parish life at that time, we may take it that very little really amiss escaped detection.

There were obviously 'campaigns' against particular faults at particular times, to the almost entire neglect of other faults which could not have been so entirely absent. In the present records many types of case normally dealt with in church courts do not occur at all.

The Administration of the Peculiar of Stratford

Before the Reformation, the peculiar jurisdiction was exercised by the Warden of the College of Stratford-upon-Avon. The College had been founded in 1331 and was suppressed in 1546. By the Charter granted to the Borough in 1553, the exercise of the jurisdiction passed to the Vicar of Stratford. From 1619 onwards this right was the subject of dispute with the Consistory Court of Worcester.[5]

As already stated, for two years out of every three — during the period under consideration — the Stratford Peculiar Court was independent of the Bishop of Worcester. Every third year, therefore, there would be no sessions to record. In fact, there appears to have been no regular sequence to the 'inhibited' years, and it cannot be said with certainty which years were administered by the Consistory Court. The Act Books of the Bishop of Worcester, which do survive for a good proportion of the period,[6] should, theoretically, include cases from Stratford approximately every third year, but there is no clear evidence of this. It may well be, indeed, that for the inhibited years the Vicar himself was appointed as the Bishop's 'commissary', and in any case a separate record — now lost — might have been kept.

The Stratford Church Court Act Books, 1590 to 1625

The two books containing these records, described bibliographically on page 117, are respectively of 74 and 70 pages.

The first is evidently the fortuitous survival of the record of occasional sessions of the court, sometimes a group of consecutive ones, but with long gaps, between 1590 and 1608, with a single session in 1616. The second is a full record of sessions for just two years, 1622 and 1624.

The court sat about once a month, the year often commencing with the important annual (or occasionally bi-annual) Visitation or inspection. Of the sessions recorded those of 8 July 1600, 25 November 1602, 13 April 1608, 24 May 1622, 11 May 1624 and 3 May 1625 are specifically described as Visitations; the remainder, if at all, as 'Acts'.

The earliest sessions recorded are those for November and December, 1590, and these, separated by six blank pages, are followed by ones for October 1592 and February 1592/3. An intervening court session, in December 1592, is obliquely referred to, and it is probable that the clerk of the court often found it easier to annotate earlier session records than to make fresh entries.

The next sessions to be recorded, although on consecutive

pages, are single ones for October 1595, July 1600 and November 1602.

Two blank pages are followed by the long session of early May 1606 (of which the start appears to be missing), with a reference to one in July, then sessions in December 1606, February and March 1606/7. Apart from a brief entry for 31 March 1607 that year is missing entirely, and then we have a splendid series of nine consecutive monthly sessions from April to December 1608. This effectively ends the book, but what was evidently a blank page between the August and October 1608 sessions has been utilised seven years later for the all-important single session of 26 March 1616.

The second book is maintained very differently. Although only covering the years 1622 and 1624, for these it forms a complete record. Each year commences with a Visitation in May, and ten and eight other sessions respectively are recorded, concluding with the Visitation in May 1625. Although not always monthly, they are clearly consecutive.

The many gaps in the first volume cannot be accounted for by the inhibited years to Worcester, though there is a possibility that 1591, and a probability that 1607 and 1623, were – as these are missing years at times that the books appear to have been better maintained. It can be seen that only in 1608, 1622 and 1624 do we get a complete picture of the court's working – but fortunately, preferable though it would of course be to have fuller records surviving, particularly for the years of Shakespeare's residence in Stratford, those scattered session records that do survive serve together to give us a very representative picture of its activities and their effect.

Language and Spelling

These records are of great value also because they give copious examples of the language in use at Stratford in Shakespeare's time and provide a good idea of Shakespeare's pronunciation. The clerk of the court, fortunately, often used English to record the evidence, and his spelling, like that of everyone else then, even the most educated, was phonetic; he spelt as he spoke. And Shakespeare's speech, like everyone else's, of whatever class, was that of his locality.[7] So when we read aloud what the clerk wrote, we hear the accents of a Stratford man, a contemporary of Shakespeare, who spoke just as Shakespeare did.

In the matter of the spelling of Shakespeare's name, it is interesting to note that the clerk of the Church Court used the form 'Shakespeere' for the poet's daughter Susanna, and both 'Shakespere' and 'Shaxpeare' for his brother Richard.[8] The six surviving signatures of the poet himself all begin with 'Shaks-', so that it is virtually certain that Shakespeare's own pronunciation, and the Stratford pronunciation of the name, used a short 'a'.

In Shakespeare's time the written literary language was probably nearer to the spoken language than ever before or since. Professor F.P. Wilson attributed to Shakespeare an instinct for what was permanent in the colloquial language of the day, stronger than that of any contemporary dramatist; and he believed that the conditions of the art of the drama did not allow Shakespeare to stray far from the popular idiom, and even if they had, that his mind was of a cast that would still have found the material upon which it worked mainly in the diction of common life.[9] The clerk's entries in English provide a useful series for linguistic study. In the Calendar, therefore, these are given in full, retaining the original spelling, though the punctuation is modern.

Christian Names

These records taken with other local records, particularly the Parish Registers, show that the Christian names in use at Stratford in Shakespeare's time were for the most part common names like John, Robert, Richard and William; Alice, Margaret, Elizabeth and Anne. This is borne out by other contemporary local records. There are no fanciful names such as Professor Claude Jenkins found in a Taunton Court Act Book of about this date (1624),[10] such as Surmina, Petronilla, Sidwella and Kenburga.

A few names were out of the ordinary and of recent introduction into this country. These included the biblical ones which came in with the Reformation: Daniel, Abraham, Isaac, Matthew, Paul and Zachary (shortened to Zache). Shakespeare's two daughters had scriptural names. The books of Susanna and Judith were both included in the Geneva version of the Bible, with which in his plays Shakespeare shows considerable acquaintance.

On the other hand some names like Simon and Clement went out with the Reformation: only two Simons and one Clement occur here.

Alexander, Giles, Hercules, Julius (in the form July), Vincent, Charles and Ursula were names of rare occurrence anywhere in England at this time; and the anglicised form of Lewis for Ludovicus had not come into general use.[11]

As for surnames, *aliases* or alternatives were more often found than today. There are various explanations of this and it is almost always impossible to be certain which one applies to any particular instance. Women sometimes used their unmarried names as an alternative to that of their husbands, as they still do in Scotland. In both sexes, however, an *alias* may indicate a complete change of name, or bastardy or a place of origin or a nickname or an occupation.

REFERENCES

1   The oath whereby an accused person might be required to answer directly to questions concerning his guilt.

2   Excommunication was a terrific sentence which had fallen into largely routine use. It had become the formal consequence of disobedience to any order of the court, from the initial order to appear before it, onwards.

3   Christopher Hill, *Society and Puritanism in Pre-Revolutionary England* (1964), Chapter 7, 'The Bawdy Courts'.

4 The percentage of those who obeyed citation either at once or shortly after are as follows: for the first Act Book, 65%; for the second, 62%. Compare the statistics and comments, the result of a wide survey, in R.A. Marchant, *The Church under the Law . . . 1560 to 1640* (1969), especially Chapter 6, 'Church Discipline'.

5 For a short notice of the history of the Peculiar see P. Styles, 'The Borough of Stratford-upon-Avon', *The Victoria History of the County of Warwick*, vol. 3 (1945).

6 Worcestershire Record Office, ref. 794-011. The surviving years are 1590-93, 1599-1603, 1607-25. For this period alone there are nine volumes, each of many hundreds of pages, covering the whole diocese, totally unindexed. These will be examined for the prospective full edition of the Stratford Act Books.

7 See H.C. Wyld, *A History of Modern Colloquial English* (reprint of 1956), pp.109, 110.

8 Sir E.K. Chambers noted 83 variations of the spelling. See *William Shakespeare*, vol. 2, Appendix E, 'The Name Shakespeare'.

9 F.P. Wilson, Annual Shakespeare Lecture, *Proceedings of the British Academy*, vol. 27 (1941).

10 Ed. C. Jenkins, *The Act Book of the Archdeacon of Taunton, 1624*, Somerset Record Society, vol. 43 (1928).

11 E.G. Withycombe, *The Oxford Dictionary of English Christian Names* (reprint of 1963).

PART III

THE CASES

THE BACKGROUND TO THE CASES:
MAIN LANDMARKS IN SHAKESPEARE'S LIFE

AS A PRELIMINARY and to serve as a background to a description of the types of cases it is interesting to associate the dates of the major court sittings in the Act Book for 1590 to 1616 with main landmarks in Shakespeare's life and the usually accepted dates of the writing of some of the plays.[1]

1564 - 26 April	Baptism of Shakespeare at Stratford-upon-Avon.
1582 - 27 November	Entry in Register of Bishop of Worcester of special licence for the marriage with only one asking of banns between William Shakespeare and Anne Whateley of Temple Grafton, Warwickshire.
1582 - 28 November	Fulke Sandells and John Richardson, farmers of Stratford, entered into a bond exempting the Bishop of Worcester from all liability should the marriage of William Shakespeare and Anne Hathaway prove unlawful.[2]
1583 - 26 May	Susanna, daughter, baptised.
1584/5 - 2 February	Hamnet and Judith, son and daughter, baptised.
1590-1	Parts 1, 2 and 3 of *Henry VI*.
1592	By this date Shakespeare was apparently a successful dramatist in London. But he remained

deeply attached to his native place and paid fairly frequent visits to it.

1595	*Romeo and Juliet*; *Richard II*.
1597	Shakespeare purchased New Place, the second largest and one of the finest houses in Stratford.
1600	*As You Like It*; *Twelfth Night*; *Julius Caesar*; *Hamlet*.
1606	*King Lear*; *Macbeth*.
1607 - 5 June	Marriage of Susanna, daughter, to Dr. John Hall.
1608	*Pericles*.
1610	The date when Shakespeare is generally assumed to have settled at New Place in Stratford-upon-Avon. *The Winter's Tale*.
1611	*The Tempest*.
1615/6 - 10 February	Marriage of Judith Shakespeare to Thomas Quiney.
1616 - 25 March	Shakespeare signed his will.
- 23 April	Death of Shakespeare at New Place.
- 25 April	Burial of Shakespeare in the Parish Church.

REFERENCES

1 For the life I follow E.K. Chambers, *William Shakespeare* (1930), vol. 2, pp.xiv-xv; and for the plays F.E. Halliday, *A Shakespeare Companion* (1952), pp.584-587.

2 Shakespeare's marriage is discussed on pages 87-88; and see E.K. Chambers, *op. cit.*, vol. 2, pp.41-52.

THE VARIOUS TYPES OF CASE

WE TAKE as examples cases which directly concern Shakespeare and those near to him, or which otherwise help to re-create the Stratford of Shakespeare's day. For convenience the cases are classified under their various types.

Family relationships are established mostly from the printed Parish Register, details of which are in the Select Book List.

The formal parts of the court proceedings are necessarily somewhat repetitive: but the repetitions are worth bearing with since they represent as nothing else can a vital part of the actualities of the time: what had, in fact, to be borne with in everyday life.

Quotations from the original Act Books are given in this Section in modern spelling and with modern punctuation.

ATTENDANCE AT CHURCH

ATTENDANCE AT CHURCH was demanded of all adults by the law of both church and state. It is likely, however, that the authorities in Stratford as in other places may have been reluctant to press the matter too far. As Dr. Marchant points out, the effect of presenting non-attenders was all too often merely to turn them into excommunicates. 'It is for this reason', he says, 'that one suspects that church attendance, particularly on summer afternoons, was much less than the hundred per cent of fit persons envisaged by the law'.[1] At Stratford, taking the years which are represented in any degree of fulness in the records before us, namely 1606, 1608, 1622 and 1624, it may be said that far less than one per cent of the liable population came under the charge of absence from church.

Churchwardens and sidesmen were directed to levy 12 pence upon all absentees for each absence. How far this was observed in the country generally is still a matter for enquiry. It is particularly interesting, therefore, to find here an example of insistence on the levy, and that two sidesmen, not wardens, were charged. William Wylitt and John Smythe were before the court on 10 October 1592 because 'they levy not the 12d. of such as absent themselves from church according to the statute'. They were ordered to certify on *each* court day that they had collected it.

People were also bound to remain in church until the end of the service. Joan Tawnte, appearing in court on 8 December 1590, confessed 'that she useth not to stay in the church in service time and sermon time' and 'that she at her going out of the church with beckoning with her finger and laughing also for swearing by the name of God'. For this she had to acknowledge her fault in the parish church 'in the face of the church in her accustomed clothing'.

Thomas Court was reported as 'a common goer out of church in prayer and sermon time' and upon appearing on 24 October 1622 made matters worse for he 'swore by the name of God' twice. But he soon submitted and upon petitioning the favour of the court he was dismissed with a monition. Katherine Brookes, widow, and Zachary Tandy were on the same day also charged with leaving church. She 'saith that it was but one time that she did so and promiseth to amend that fault hereafter'. Tandy also promised amendment.

REFERENCE
1   R.A. Marchant, *The Church under the Law . . . 1560-1640* (1969), p.218.

NON-RECEPTION OF THE HOLY COMMUNION

IN THIS PERIOD every man and woman in the country was bound by the rubric of the Book of Common Prayer and had to receive the Holy Communion three times a year of which Easter had to be one.

The great majority obeyed. A large proportion of those who did not were either avowed Catholics or had strong Catholic sympathies, 'church papists' as they were called, people who were prepared to attend the ordinary Sunday and holy-day services of the Church of England in order to avoid the penalties of the law, but who drew the line at receiving the Holy Communion. 'Church papists' existed in large numbers though it is impossible to estimate their strength with any exactitude.[1]

Under Elizabeth I, if church papists could individually satisfy their consciences all was well with them: they attended the services and so avoided the fines. For the Queen firmly refused to allow anyone to be required to receive the communion as a test of loyalty.[2] In the early years of James they remained similarly unmolested.

Then in November 1605 came the discovery of the Gunpowder Plot. Immediately the government greatly increased the severity of the law against Catholics and for the first time clamped down on church papists. An Act of Parliament was passed mentioning particularly those who 'adhere in their hearts to the popish religion', but who 'do nevertheless the better to hide their false hearts repair sometimes to the church to escape the penalty of the Law'. All now had to receive the Holy Communion at least once in the year on penalty of a £20 fine in the first year, £40 in the second year and £60 in each succeeding year, and constables had to present to Quarter Sessions the names of all papists absent from communion.[3]

The church authorities were in consequence increasingly vigilant. Anyone who did not receive the communion would be suspected of being a Catholic or at least of having strong Catholic sympathies.

It is in the light of these new stringent regulations that we must view the citation of 21 persons before the Stratford church court early in May 1606 for not receiving the communion at the previous Easter (Easter Day in that year fell on 20 April). This has every appearance of being the result of a campaign since there are only three other charges of non-reception spread over all the years covered by this first Act Book (1590-1616).

Almost certainly, then, these 21 Stratfordians may be written down either as avowed Catholics or as church papists. This is borne out by such facts as are available concerning certain of them.

Margaret Reynolds was the wife of Thomas Reynolds, gentleman, an avowed Catholic who paid his monthly fines for recusancy. The Reynolds family lived in Colles Farm overlooking the Church Way, and also in Chapel Street, in the house now the northern part of the *Shakespeare Hotel*. Two years before this court sitting Thomas and Margaret Reynolds had given refuge to a fugitive Jesuit priest disguised as a layman. They were friends of Shakespeare who bequeathed to their son 26s. 8d. to buy a memorial ring.[4]

Sibil Cawdrey was the widow of Ralph Cawdrey, butcher, who had shops in Middle Row in Bridge Street and was tenant of the *Angel* inn at the top of the street. One of the Cawdreys' sons was a priest of the Jesuit order.[5]

John Wheeler senior had been presented for recusancy back in 1592, along with John Shakespeare, the poet's father, and others.[6]

Four of this group of 21 put forward excuses which were

common form among church papists: so much so that the
clerk cut short his quoting of their excuses with a cynical
'etc.'.

George Hollis appeared for his wife and said she did not
receive 'because she was not in charity etc.'. Robert Brookes
pleaded that 'there was dissension between him and his
brothers etc.'.[7]

Edward Powell answering for his wife said she did not
receive 'on account of poverty etc.'. Hamlet Sadler, speaking
no doubt also for his wife Judith who was charged with
him, 'petitioned time to cleanse his conscience': and this
time there is no 'etc.'. He and his wife, the godparents of
Shakespeare's twins, obviously abstained on principle and
he used the stock phrase to express it.

All the 21, with the exception of Isabella Whitbred, are
entered as having made their appearance either at once or
at a sitting soon after; and as having been dismissed.[8] Ten
of these are stated to have received the communion. The
others, since they were dismissed, may be assumed to
have done so.

The most interesting of these non-receivers is William
Shakespeare's daughter Susanna. She was one of those
who did not answer the first summons and the penalty of
her disobedience was reserved to the next court. There is
no record of her being called again, merely the clerk's note
of dismissal in the margin. This probably means that she
made a later appearance and that she satisfied the Judge
by receiving the communion or by promising to do so.

Although Susanna Shakespeare appears among Stratford
church papists we cannot be absolutely certain that she was
indeed one of them. But it certainly looks like it; and the
fact that in the following year she married a prominent
local protestant in Dr. John Hall does not tell against this
conclusion, for religion at that time was not of necessity
socially divisive.

The case against Susanna adds a little more material for
speculation on the religion of Shakespeare himself. He

Fig. 3. *GEORGE VERTUE'S DRAWING OF NEW PLACE*

Shakespeare bought this house, the second largest in the town, and lived there from 1610 until his death in 1616. Described by Leland as 'a pretty house of brick and timber'; it had previously been owned by Sir Hugh Clopton, the builder of the great bridge over the Avon. New Place was demolished in 1702. Only the site and gardens remain, preserved as a memorial to the poet by the Shakespeare Memorial Trust.

This drawing by George Vertue, from memory in 1737, is the only known representation of Shakespeare's house. It is among the Portland Papers deposited in the British Museum and it is reproduced here by kind permission of His Grace the Duke of Portland. See the interesting article on this drawing by Frank Simpson, in Shakespeare Survey, 5 (1952).

would probably be in sympathy with his daughter and his friends the Sadlers on human grounds, and possibly at least in a measure, on higher grounds also.

It has recently been suggested that the existence within the Church of England of a body of church papists may have influenced the growth of 'anglo-catholic' views at the expense of 'protestant' traditions in the later 16th and early 17th centuries.[9] It is intriguing to think of Susanna and perhaps her father as primitive anglo-catholics.

But we are left with the now widely accepted opinion that William Shakespeare was, like most of his compatriots, a man of the Establishment. Within that framework were many shades of belief and it is impossible to say which Shakespeare held.

———————

In the second Act Book (1622-25) there are six cases of non-reception. In no instance is there an entry of compliance though one, Thomas Loach, junior, did at least promise to receive (27 July 1622).

The case against John Lane is of particular interest. In the acts of the court held on 19 July 1622 before the vicar, Thomas Wilson, is the bald entry 'John Lane, gentleman, did not receive the sacrament'. He was the son of John Lane of Alveston Manor and nephew of John Lane, an avowed Catholic.[10] At the time of this entry he was aged 32. Nine years before, in 1613, he had been summoned to the Bishop's Court at Worcester for slandering Susanna Shakespeare, aged 30, and then of course married to Dr. Hall. Lane put it about that she 'had the running of the reins and had been naught(y) with Ralph Smith at John Palmer's'. Lane ignored the citation, incurred excommunication and Susanna's character was thereby cleared.[11]

In 1619 Lane led the protest in Stratford against the appointment of the puritan Thomas Wilson as vicar. So the feuding in these little towns went on.[12]

REFERENCES

1   W.R. Trimble, *The Catholic Laity under Elizabeth I* (Cambridge, Mass., 1964), pp.102-4; see also J. Bossy, 'The Character of Elizabethan Catholicism', *Past and Present*, no. 21 (1962).

2   P. McGrath, *Papists and Puritans under Elizabeth I* (1967) p.117 n.1.

3   3 and 4 Jac. I, c. 4. For the text see G.W. Prothero, *Select Statutes* . . . (1906), pp.256 ff.

4   E.I. Fripp, *Shakespeare's Stratford* (1928), pp.31, 41-2.

5   E.I. Fripp, *op.cit.*, p.13.

6   E.I. Fripp, *op.cit.*, pp.15-18. Fripp and others before and after him have made John Shakespeare a protestant recusant; but there can be little doubt that a recusant at this period meant a catholic. The ecclesiastical lawyer Richard Burn sums up the matter admirably: 'To be a recusant doth not necessarily imply being a papist . . . but as there were few or no other recusants but papists at that time (i.e. of Elizabeth I and James I) they (i.e., the statutes) have regard chiefly to persons of that profession': *The Justice of the Peace* ed. 1769, vol. 3, pp.181-2.

7   See Robert Birt, *The Elizabethan Settlement of Religion* (1907), p.52, quoting British Museum, Harleian MSS., 1221, n.5: 'His (i.e. the papist's) main subtlety is to shift off the communion, for which he is never unfurnished of a quarrel, and will be sure always to be out of charity at Easter'.

8   And even in the case of Isabella Whitbred there is a large cross (X) made in the margin as there is against the names of some of those who were dismissed: this probably means that she, too, was dismissed.

9   P. McGrath, *op. cit.*, pp.29-30.

10   E.I. Fripp, *op. cit.*, pp.30-31.

11   E.K. Chambers, *William Shakespeare* (1930), vol. 2, p.12.

12   P. Styles, 'The Borough of Stratford-upon-Avon' in *The Victoria History of the County of Warwick*, vol. 3 (1945), p.281.

RECUSANCY

RECUSANTS DIFFERED from church papists in that they were avowed Catholics who refused to attend any services of the Church of England.

There are only three persons entered as recusants by that name; they occur in the second Act Book.

Mistress Frekleton was cited to the court of 8 October 1624 'for a recusant in not coming to church'. She was ordered to be cited afresh. The same injunction was repeated at four subsequent sittings, the last one being on 4 March 1624/5; and there the record leaves her.

Thomas Tailer and his wife Elizabeth of Bishopton were summoned to appear on 6 December 1624 'for recusants in not coming to the church of Bishopton this Easter year'. They did not obey; the next, and last, entry concerning them is on 21 January 1624/5 when the penalty of their contumacy was again reserved.

Named immediately after Mistress Frekleton though not specifically as a recusant was Elinor Badger 'for not coming to church'. She did not appear and was ordered to be cited afresh. She was probably a daughter or grand-daughter of the George Badger who had been a leader of the avowed Catholics of Stratford and a friend of John Shakespeare, living near him in Henley Street. It is possible that Elinor Badger was a recusant but, as often happened in such families, it is more likely that by this date she had become a church papist.[1]

REFERENCE
1 Just after the Gunpowder Plot, George Badger was found to be harbouring some incriminating relics from nearby Clopton House, a centre of the conspiracy: 'copes, vestments, crucifixes, chalices and other massing relics' in a cloakbag. See E.I. Fripp, *Shakespeare's Haunts near Stratford* (1929), p.131.

ABUSE OF SUNDAY AND HOLY DAYS

IN SHAKESPEARE'S TIME Puritanism took strong hold in Stratford. With it came strict teaching on the keeping of the Sunday, which came to be regarded as the Mosaic Sabbath. The chief exponent was Nicholas Bownde whose Book *The Doctrine of the Sabbath* appeared in 1595 and immediately found wide acceptance. From that time Sabbatarianism became a main plank in the Puritan platform. Closely associated with Bownde in the fierce controversy which followed were two local men, Nicholas and Richard Byfield, sons of Richard Byfield, vicar of Stratford, from whom they imbibed their doctrine. They were the authors of two of the most influential works in the great spate of sabbatarian literature produced in England in the early 17th century.[1]

It is particularly interesting, therefore, to follow in these records the actual conditions prevailing in puritan Stratford over the observance of Sunday in the time of the Byfields − and of Shakespeare. Here the number of cases under this head greatly outnumber those concerning sexual immorality: namely 90 as against 54.

At Stratford, as elsewhere, it was the duty of the churchwardens, helped by other officials and taken in turns, no doubt, to go round the parish during service time to see for themselves if anyone was breaking the law.[2] We may presume that the officials were also on the look-out for those who kept their shops open during service time. In the years 1590-92 there seems to have been a determined drive against this. No fewer than 31 persons were called to answer for it.

As it happens, the first name in the first Act Book is of one charged with Sabbath breaking. He is William Llewellyn, spelt Flewellyn. The character in *Henry V* immediately springs to mind; and we are at the same time reminded of how Shakespearian names occur in local documents. Besides absenting himself from church, Llewellyn 'useth to open his shop windows[3] on the Sabbath day'. He was admonished at the court session of 9 November 1590 to attend church and to desist from trading.

At the sitting on the following 8 December Richard Heath *alias* Swanne denied that he had opened his shop on Sunday and was ordered to purge himself with four neighbours. Perhaps this caused trouble in his home for he was indignant and 'persistently put forth some scandalous words in the court, saying to the Judge "You have been the cause to put me and my wife asunder", and some other words'. For this he incurred excommunication.

On the same day William Trowt, among others, appeared on the same charge. He made no fuss. He admitted the offence and was dismissed with the usual admonition. Eighteen years later Trowte was again in court (4 November 1608) for a Sunday offence, this time for drinking with others during the hours of service. Again he respectfully appeared when summoned and was directed to pay an unspecified sum to the parish poor fund. William Trowt's dwelling and shop were on the east side of High Street at the opening of the chure leading into Bridge Street. His father held the office of corporation leather sealer in 1559, at the same time as John Shakespeare was constable.[4] Trowt's daughter Katherine was later involved in a charge of fornication.

Francis Smith was a haberdasher like his father William who was Shakespeare's godfather. He lived at the corner house in Middle Row, facing the High Cross. He appeared on 10 October 1592 and was warned not to open his shop 'until evening prayer on Sundays and holy-days are finished unless from cause of necessity'. On the same day Thomas Jones, butcher, was ordered 'that he do not sell or kill any wares after the first peal to divine service until an hour after evening prayer upon the Sundays or holy days'. Robert Biddle the shoemaker and John Tomlyns the tailor with his servant were also warned over their Sunday and holy day activities. Tomlyns no doubt expressed the indignation of many on this score: he 'behaved irreverently in court, addressing the Judge, "Why may not I lie as well as you?" ' and drew upon himself thereby a formal excommunication. Ralph Lorde 'encouraged in his house in time of divine service certain persons eating and drinking' and four are named. Lorde and all the rest except one appeared and were told not to do it again. The absentee, William Sampson, incurred excommunication.

But Lorde seems to have been incorrigible. On 28 February 1606/7 he was again before the court 'for the misuse of Sunday in the selling of meat in the time of divine service'. He appeared and was let off with an admonition. Yet again he appeared on 4 November 1608 with a round half-dozen other men 'for drinking on the Sabbath day in prayer time'. This time they were dismissed upon payment of a certain unspecified sum for the use of the poor of the parish.

Robert Johnson also entertained during church time 'divers parties playing at cards and George Shingleton drinking'. Like the others who behaved themselves in court he escaped with a monition (13 February 1592/3).

In the court acts for 1 October 1595 we find an isolated case of Sunday gaming, though surely it could not have been the only one at the time. John Smith and 'George' (no surname is given), the hostler of the *Bear* at the bottom of Bridge Street, were before the court for playing quoits in service time. No action or monition is recorded against them.

At courts held in October, November and December, 1608, several men were presented for 'breaking holy days' by 'labouring with their teams' during the previous harvest season – St. Bartholomew's day (24 August) and St. Matthew's day (21 September) are specifically named. It is a measure of how the matter was regarded by the Puritan church authorities at Stratford that these substantial farmers were dismissed upon payment of a derisory penny or twopence to the use of the poor. We may infer from these ridiculously light sentences that the presentments were made as a formality and merely to comply with the church law. Parish officials were expected to report people who worked on saints' days which ardent Puritans like the Stratford men abhorred on principle. Moreover in the new industrial society which was then developing the observance of these days was beginning to be regarded by some as an intolerable hindrance to progress.

Certain of these holy-day breakers are of particular interest. Anthony Nash, described as 'gentleman' was an intimate friend of Shakespeare who left him and his brother John Nash 26s. 8d. each to buy memorial rings. Anthony was the father of Thomas Nash who married Shakespeare's granddaughter Elizabeth Hall.

The Thomas Burmans, senior and junior, and Stephen Burman, belonged to the established Shottery family; they were friends of the Hathaways there.

Thomas Reynolds, entered as 'gentleman', was head of a wealthy Catholic family, the husband of Margaret who also appears in our records (see under **Non-Reception of Holy Communion**, page 45). He lived in Chapel Street and also was by Shakespeare's will another of the recipients of 26s. 8d. for the purchase of a ring.

John Gibbs, 'gentleman', and his brother Richard lived on the west side of Rother Street just opposite the entrance to Ely Street.

Robert Monmouth and John Sheffield, as Churchwardens in 1600 and 1601, signed each page of the Parish Register to that date, when the customary transcript of the old register was made in 1600.

The age-old festivities of May Day sometimes clashed with the feast day of St. Philip and St. James which fell on 1 May. John Allen appeared in court on 28 May 1622 'for dancing the morris in Evening Prayer time on the feast day of Phillip and Jacob'. Although he promised that he would 'never commit the like again' he was ordered to do penance before the whole congregation and there to repeat the promise. But he did not obey. A little later he was charged 'because he hath not confessed his fault and since that time he hath committed the like offence again'. He was enjoined 'that the next Sabbath day presently [i.e. immediately] after the reading of the Gospel, he confess his fault in the middle aisle that the congregation may take notice of it'. Five others charged with Allen were similarly directed. These cases show how the strait-laced authorities regarded these holiday junketings and the licence that went with them, for that is what bothered them, not the fact that a holy day had been broken. It seems strange that Francis Palmer, servant to John Hobbins of Shottery, 'for being the Maid Marrian' at the same time is merely noted as 'pardoned'; but perhaps this was because he was under age. Girls' parts were then played by boys.

On 28 October 1622 Thomas Canning stood before the court 'for profaning the Sabbath day' and admitted 'that he did play at ball ... and that it was the first time he so did and doth promise that it shall be the last', and submitted himself to the correction of the Judge. Nothing more is added but he probably received the same kindly treatment as William Davis who also appeared on that day 'for fishing on the Sabbath' and was pardoned with a monition.

Even with the strict standards prevailing at Stratford, it would seem that, as elsewhere, the court was prepared to be reasonable over minor breakings of the Sabbath. Robert Wotton, blacksmith, appearing on 3 August 1622, 'for grinding of scythes on the Sabbath day', upon pleading 'that it was upon necessity that he did it', and promising not to repeat the offence, was dismissed with a monition. George Robbins and Oliver Sandells for playing cards during Evening Prayer time on Sunday were ordered on 31 January 1622/3 to acknowledge their misdemeanour in church semi-privately before the minister and the churchwardens. Sandells was a son of Fulke Sandells, the friend of Shakespeare's youth who in 1582 was one of the sureties for his marriage bond at Worcester. The year before that he was an overseer of Richard Hathaway's will and answerable for paying Anne Hathaway £6 13s. 4d. on the day she married.

At the court sitting held on 3 September 1624 John Mace 'for suffering drunkenness and fighting with much other disorder in his house on the Sabbath day in time of prayer' had to make acknowledgment before the magistrate as well as the minister and churchwardens and further to pay 12 pence to the use of the poor. He evidently obeyed; yet for not paying the fees incurred in the proceedings he was excommunicated. Eventually he settled up, as the clerk's note in the margin informs us: 'received 8d. for Mr. Wilson', that is, the Judge of the court, the Vicar.

REFERENCES

1 See Byfield, Richard and Nicholas, in *Dictionary of National Biography*.

2 See section on **Churchwardens and Sidesmen**, page 24.

3 'Window' meant a shutter of some kind. See *New (Oxford) English Dictionary*.

4 *Minutes and Accounts . . . 1553-1620* (Introduction and notes by E.I. Fripp), vol. 1, p.xlvi.

MISBEHAVIOUR IN CHURCH AND CHURCHYARD

JUDGING FROM the court records it would seem, at any rate, that upon the whole behaviour in church was exemplary. And there were no disputes or rows over seats: none of the vicious pin-jabbing, shoving-up, pushing off or provocative sitting on laps sometimes found in other places. In the churchyard, too, it would appear that Stratfordians comported themselves with equal decorum.

There are only four cases of misbehaviour in church, two in each of the Act Books, and they all concern men. This is unusual. The sexes sat apart in those days and it was most often among the women that trouble arose.

On 13 May 1608 Robert Willson and Matthew Martyn were called for unspecified 'irreverence in time of divine service'. Neither appeared immediately and both had formal excommunication entered against them. 'Thereafter', however, they submitted, petitioned the favour of the court, listened to the admonition of the judge about good behaviour in church and secured dismissal.

The other two cases, happily, go into some detail and help to conjure up a picture of what might occur during a long-drawn-out sermon on a hot day.

Richard Baker, shoemaker, appeared on 28 May 1622 'for striking in the church in time of sermon, namely for striking the son of John Rogers of Shottery . . . and saith that the boy was playing and keeping a noise, that the said Richard could not hear what the preacher said; and the said Richard did admonish the boy to desist but he would not. And thereupon the said Richard did give the said boy a little tap upon the head'. The Judge admonished him 'that from henceforth he strike no more; but if such offence be in the church, he shall complain to the magistrate, that such boys may be whipped'. Baker was thereupon dismissed.

At the same session, Edward Rogers answered a citation 'for striking the servant of William Castle, glover, in church in sermon time'. (It must have been excessively tedious that day.) He admitted 'that he did swing the boy by the ear because the said boy did fight and jostle with another boy and disturb the congregation'. Rogers was also ordered in future to report naughty boys to the magistrate.

Boys punished for mischief of this kind were probably dealt with by the beadle more or less privately, not at the High Cross whipping post which was for rogues and vagabonds and prostitutes.

NEGLECT OF THE CATECHISM

SHAKESPEARE in his plays shows close acquaintance with the Book of Common Prayer; and like most of his contemporaries he no doubt had the Catechism contained in it by heart. The rubric in the Prayer Book laid down strict instructions that all were to learn it. Thus it became an integral part of the spiritual and mental equipment of every man.

The Catechism which Shakespeare learnt was the same as that in the present Prayer Book, though it extended only as far as the section on the Lord's Prayer. The remainder was added at the beginning of James I's reign and young Stratfordians would have to get that up as well. The all-important and pervading Canons of 1603,[1] summing up previous instructions, directed that in every parish the minister was to instruct the children, young people, servants and apprentices for half an hour or more before Evening Prayer every Sunday in the Ten Commandments, the Creed and the Lord's Prayer and was to teach and examine them in the Catechism; and further that all parents, masters and mistresses were to see that those in their care attended church for the purpose.

There was in some areas a certain latitude in the interpretation of the Canons. But everywhere articles of enquiry made a point of asking how the duties over Catechism were carried out and on the whole the authorities were insistent on obedience.

Negligence by the clergy in catechising was often associated with a low standard of education on their part. At Stratford this certainly did not apply. The vicars and curates were all men of relatively high academic attainment. There are no cases against any of them.

As to the laity there are no cases in the first Act Book. In the Visitations of 1622 and 1624, however, there is the reflection of what appears to have been a determined drive against slackness. 29 persons were cited in connection with catechism offences. This rather large number may be compared with the very low figures found at or about the same time in the few other places for which they are available.

At the court session of 24 October 1622 Thomas Hornby, blacksmith, was reported 'for not sending his children and servants to be catechised'. He duly appeared and was enjoined to send them to church 'upon Sunday senight next coming'. At the same time John Harding, musician, appeared for the same omission and was ordered as Hornby. There is no subsequent entry and it may be assumed that they complied. Hornby was of the smithy in Henley Street, a neighbour of the Shakespeares. Harding is a welcome addition to the few other Stratford musicians of the time already known: Thomas Clark the taborer, John Knowles the minstrel, and the blind harpist whom the young Philip Sidney heard singing Percy and Douglas ballads at Chipping Norton.[2]

On 24 October, among a number of young people who appeared for not going to be catechised were Thomas West, currier, Robert Wheeler, glover and Thomas Swanne, shoemaker. They were probably apprentices.

In these catechism cases as in others, the clerk has often not bothered to write up all the stages of the procedure. Sometimes he notes 'pardoned' or 'dismissed'; sometimes not. We may assume, however, remembering the checks and balances of the time, that mostly people came to heel. But not always.

This is to be seen in the case of William Bartlett which we can follow in some detail. He was cited for 22 May 1624 'for refusing to come to be catechised'. He did not appear and therefore incurred excommunication which is duly entered in the acts. Bartlett afterwards attended and the clerk writes that the apparitor 'upon his oath hath delivered that the said

William Bartlett did, when he was cited, speak reproachful and reviling words of this court, namely "Shit upon the court" '. For this outburst he was ordered to do public penance in his ordinary apparel during Morning Prayer on the following Sunday, standing in the middle aisle until the end of the sermon; 'and also to come diligently to be catechised hereafter every Sabbath day until he can answer the minister in the principles of the Christian religion'. The session of 16 July, however, found Bartlett still recalcitrant and he was ordered to be cited 'by ways and means'. On 3 September he was entered 'for not answering the questions in the catechism and also presented for a fame of incontinency with Katherine Trowt'. Over the incontinence he was ordered to purge himself with four others at the next court. He obeyed. On 6 December he appeared bringing with him the four compurgators, who, as usual, are named and he was dismissed. As for the catechism, the record leaves us to guess.

Sometimes good excuses could be offered; but the court, though tolerant, was pertinacious. On 3 August 1622 in answer to the detection 'for not coming to be catechised, being warned to the same', Richard Fransicar of Shottery pleaded 'that he would have come but his master William Richardson would not suffer him but did send him about his business two Sundays together'. The Judge gave him a specific order: 'to come to be publicly catechised upon Sunday the 11 of August and to certify the same'. Very likely he obeyed like the others called at the same time. We may infer this because the clerk was content to jot down in the margin against Fransicar's name 'call him to Worcester for fees or his master', omitting the note of dismissal which appears by the names of most of the rest.

One of these was William Johnsons, entered as 'of the Swan'. He was perhaps one of the boys working at the famous inn. Another was William Ingram, interesting as showing that sons of prominent families were not exempt from catechism: his father leased the fishing ground beyond the weir on the Avon.

REFERENCES
1 Canon 59.
2 See E.I. Fripp, *Shakespeare's Stratford,* p.29.

BLASPHEMY

THE EXTENT and flavour of the blasphemies and oaths to which the profane or exasperated might be driven in Shakespeare's Stratford may be caught from the few outbursts encountered here.

Joan Tawnte (what a name) offended by going out of church during service 'with beckoning with her finger and laughing and also swearing by the name of God'. She admitted the offence on 8 December 1590 and was ordered to acknowledge it on the following Sunday 'in the face of the church in her accustomed clothing'.

'God's wounds', cried Elizabeth Wheeler, using an old Catholic oath still in currency — the Queen used it. She was before the court on 1 October 1595 for brawling and abuse, obviously one of the hoydens of the parish. Still she ranted on: 'a plague of God on you all, a fart of one's arse for you'. The outraged Judge declared her excommunicated. Wheeler would be lucky if she was not dealt with by the justices as well: they had the ducking stool (kept near the Gaol in High Street) or the riverside for scolds like her.

Edward Samon was on 28 May 1622 presented 'for a common swearer'. The clerk noted 'he is the hayward of Loxley', near Stratford, and all we know is that he incurred a formal excommunication for not appearing on his first citation.

John Lupton was not only 'a common swearer' but a general nuisance besides, 'a railer, a slanderer and disordered person'. Nothing is entered against his name (19 July 1622) except the word 'pardoned', obviously added later, though the usual processes must have been gone through.

Far more serious was the offence of Eleanor Silvester, reported for 'blaspheming the name of God and saying that

God doth dote and knew not what he did, with many other blasphemous speeches and cursed oaths'. She admitted it at her appearance on 22 May 1624 and had to do penance, probably a heavy one, though no details are recorded.

On the same day Stephen Lea had to answer 'for singing profane and filthy songs, scoffing and deriding of ministers and the profession of religion'. He promised to curb his tongue but had to acknowledge the fault publicly in church during service.

SORCERY

AT THIS TIME belief in witches was firmly held. It was based upon scriptural and literary traditions, inextricably mixed with age-old traditions of the countryside, ancient counter-charms against witches and ancient methods of testing for witchcraft. The white witch was a commonplace of country life and people were even proud of their local wise woman. It was not until the ferocious witch hunts had developed that all witches were regarded as black and condemned.

It is noteworthy that in these Stratford records there are no direct cases of sorcery. Most likely the churchwardens were loath to present what they regarded as a normal, legitimate part of life. Cases of this kind in church courts anywhere appear to have been few. Churchwardens resorted to excuses as at Kings's Sutton in the Peculiar of Banbury. There, in 1619, the wardens reported that 'for witchcraft, sorcery, charms and helps for people and cattle, we can say somewhat, but for the more perfecting of our presentment we crave time till the next Visitation'.[1]

An echo of local Stratford witchcraft appears, however, in the case against Alice Parker who was summoned to the court of 14 October 1608 for abusing Elizabeth Bromley. Two other women, Susan Dart and Elenor Samon, bore testimony against Parker and she was ordered to acknowledge her fault publicly in church on the following Sunday. The abuse was perhaps understandable for the object of it was none other than 'Goody' Bromley, well known as 'an ill-look woman', a witch who could cast the evil eye. From other sources we learn that she threatened to 'overlook' the wife of Adrian Holder (who, incidentally appears elsewhere in our records in a marriage case) and bade her 'get her home' (that is, to hell) or she would 'brush the motes forth of her dirty gown'.[2]

REFERENCES

1 *The Churchwardens' Presentments in the Oxfordshire Peculiars of Dorchester, Thame and Banbury*, ed. S.A. Peyton, Oxon. Rec. Soc., vol. 10 (1928), p.299.

2 E.I. Fripp, *Shakespeare's Stratford*, p.76.

STANDING EXCOMMUNICATE AND CONSORTING
WITH EXCOMMUNICATES

SEVERAL PEOPLE were faced with the charge of allowing themselves to remain under the ban of excommunication, that is, of taking no steps to obtain absolution: they had, in technical language, allowed the excommunication to become 'aggravated' (the word is used two or three times) and so had incurred the penalty of an almost complete boycott, secular and spiritual, and rendered themselves liable, at least, to arrest by the secular arm. Against some names the clerk later noted that matters had been put right. This was probably so with most of them eventually; in small jurisdictions like Stratford, where the authorities could keep an eye on every single person, there were no doubt far fewer who defied the sentence than in other places. To stand excommunicated for long periods was not unusual; and it was certainly no new thing, for it had been fairly common in medieval times.

Those who obstinately remained excommunicate for 40 days were by law liable to be handed over to the secular authorities for imprisonment until they made submission. In practice a much longer period usually elapsed before this drastic action was taken; for one thing it was a very expensive process. There are no examples of it in the present records.

Presentments for consorting with excommunicates are rarely found anywhere. The solitary case of Thomas Woodward at Stratford is therefore worth following through. On 28 May 1622 he stood before the court 'for keeping company with William Bromley who standeth aggravated and the said Thomas hath been heretofore admonished in court several times to desist from the same'. Woodward admitted the charge and was ordered 'that upon the next Sabbath day he confess his fault in the time of divine service in the parish church before the whole congregation and there to promise amendment on pain of excommunucation'. On 29 July he was called to give reason why he had not done the penance, and, not appearing, was excommunicated. On 3 August he is entered 'for being in alehouses in prayer time on the Sabbath day'. Again he ignored the summons and excommunication was renewed. The last we hear of him is on 24 October when, being called to give reason why he stood excommunicated, he still did not appear.

We do not know what William Bromley's original offence was. The first, and only, entry about him is on 28 May, the day for which Woodward was first cited. Then he was called with four others to give reason why he stood under the sentence of aggravated excommunication, and was ordered to be cited again. William Bromley was the grandson of Matthew Bromley who lived in Rother Market and was in the leather trade. John Shakespeare, the poet's father, once had to sue him for debt.[1]

REFERENCE
1 *Minutes and Accounts . . . 1553-1620,* vol. 1, p.xlv.

ABUSE, SCANDAL, DEFAMATION

PERSONAL ABUSE and scandalmongering and defamation were no doubt regretfully accepted as an inevitable part of everyday life. But sometimes limits were exceeded, offenders were presented and the court took action.

The case of John Whode (or Wood) is for several reasons of particular interest. There was a 'public fame', or widespread strong rumour, that Wood was 'a maker of slanderous libels'. He appeared on 10 October 1592 and upon denying the charge was ordered purgation with six others, who had to be married people, at the next court. On that day, 18 December, Wood duly appeared and 'from causes moving the mind of the Judge' (the regular formula used in certain special cases) he was allowed to purge himself on his own oath alone, that is, his declaration of innocence was accepted without corroboration.

The question arises: was Wood the apparitor of that name who 11 years later is found in our records citing several people to the court? And was he an apparitor at the time of the charge? It seems very likely so. The wording of the charge, the number and married status of the compurgators, the decision of the Judge, all suggest this. The Stratford apparitors appear to have been local men.

The charge against Wood was one not infrequently brought against apparitors, whether they deserved it or not. Some, of course, did trump up accusations: as they lived on fees, the more cases they brought in the better. And everywhere the administration of the law was by modern reckoning corrupt.

Edward Latymer's is one of the very few contentious cases in the present records. He appeared for himself on 28 February 1606/7 in a cause of defamation against John Hastings,

Thomas Aynge, Richard Maio and Francis Cooke, of whom Aynge and Cooke were prominent people in Stratford. Shortly afterwards Latymer confessed that he had had carnal copulation with a certain unnamed woman; but he said he would produce Francis Hornby and Elizabeth his wife, two more well-known Stratfordians, to testify 'concerning the cause of defamation'. It looks as though Latymer was something of a blusterer: the case ends with the clerk's note that he had fled and that the others accordingly had been dismissed.

Isabell Bayles defamed Matthew Bayles — a relative perhaps[1] — and his wife Joan, calling him a cuckold and her an adulteress. ('Wittol! — Cuckold! the devil himself hath not such a name').[2] Appearing on 10 August 1608 she was ordered to acknowledge the transgression in church on the following Sunday. She petitioned the favour of the court and got excused the penance on condition that she made satisfaction to the injured couple there and then in open court by admitting that her accusations were untrue. This she did and was dismissed.

The case of Alice Parker, called on 14 October 1608 for the unspecified abuse of Elizabeth Bromley, is dealt with under the heading **Sorcery**, page 65.

Thomas Faux was evidently one whose tongue ran away with him. He made 'slanderous speeches' about Alice Brunt, 'calling her filthy whore and said he would prove her to be a whore'. He admitted (28 May 1622) 'that he called her whore but saith it was in his passion, being moved and abused by her', but denied that he said he would prove her to be one. The Judge adjourned the case. We know nothing of what transpired except that at a later hearing (19 July) Faux burst out again 'scandalizing this court by saying it was the bawdy court'.

There was a slanging match between Richard Wheeler and the wife of Richard Brooks. In court on 16 July 1624 he admitted calling her 'whore and sowlike whore, with divers other filthy speeches', but pleaded that 'the wife of Richard

Brooks calling him rogue he replied that if he were a rogue she was a whore'. For this he had to perform the relatively light penance of acknowledging the offence standing before the congregation until the end of the second lesson of Morning Prayer only, and in his ordinary clothes.

Alice Clark, presented 'for saying that Elizabeth Reynolds was Abraham Allway his whore' did not at first appear when called on 16 July 1624 but soon afterwards came and made a formal denial; whereupon she was ordered to purge herself with three others at the next court.

Anne Lane was alleged to have called Katherine Trowt just a whore — there were no elaborations. But on being called to the court on 16 July, she blurted out 'that William Bartlett hath publicly confessed before witnesses that Katherine Trowt did come to bed with him'. The churchwardens were promptly ordered to see that citations were issued against both Bartlett and Trowt.

On the same day a third case of slander came up when Katherine Shingleton appeared for calling the widow Alderne a whore and saying that all her children were bastards. She ignored the citation and so incurred excommunication. Nothing more is heard of her.

Although this was a common word of abuse, it was one particularly resented: 'to be called whore; would it not make one weep?'[3]

REFERENCES
1 The Parish Register provides no enlightenment on the relationship.
2 *The Merry Wives of Windsor*: 2: 2: 318.
3 *Othello*: 4: 2: 127.

DRUNKENNESS

DRUNKENNESS was one of the offences punished by the Justices, as well as by the church courts.

It can hardly be imagined, from the fact that only one person throughout these years was individually charged in the church court with being a drunkard, that Stratford was a place of quite exceptional sobriety. Perhaps it was a question of definition.

Thomas Clark on 24 May 1624 was detected 'for a drunkard'. He did not appear and the judge directed that he be cited anew. On 16 July he denied the charge and was ordered to purge himself with three others. Nothing more is heard of the purgation and he probably got away with it. But he failed to satisfy the court over the fees and for that he was declared excommunicate.

SEXUAL OFFENCES

THE PERMISSIVE 1970s have nothing much on the age of Shakespeare.

> Great swarms of vice worthy to be rebuked . . . outrageous seas of adultery (or breaking of wedlock), whoredom, fornication and uncleanness have not only brast in, but also overflowed the whole world . . . so abundantly that, through the customable use thereof, this vice is grown into such a height, that among many it is counted no sin at all, but rather a pastime, a dalliance and but a touch of youth; not rebuked but winked at; not punished but laughed at.

So ran the official Homily *Against Whoredom and Uncleanness*, one of those which had to be read on Sundays in every parish church when there was no sermon. And when a parson did preach on his own account, as often as not it was against the sins of the flesh that he thundered.

The church courts were regarded by the authorities as a bulwark in an age of rampant licentiousness. A preacher at St. Paul's Cross, that regular medium for official propaganda, declared that but for the courts half the children in a certain diocese would be bastards.[1]

In sexual cases people were answerable to the Justices, as well as the church courts, for such offences were looked upon as a disruption of society and deserved severe penalties. For adultery corporal punishment was sometimes ordered. This is not on record at Stratford, but what could happen may be seen from Southwell in Nottinghamshire. There the penitent being 'naked from the middle upward' the apparitor 'shall be ready with a birch rod and shall give either of the parties three stripes upon their bare shoulders'.[2]

Certainly cases of this kind formed a very large proportion of those which came before the 'bawdy Court' as it was called by the man in the street. The biting phrase turns up in various parts of the country,[3] and sure enough here it is in Stratford. We find Thomas Faux charged 'for scandalizing this court and saying it was the bawdy court'.

In spite of its prevalence, sexual immorality was viewed very seriously. It was not counted among mere rustic peccadilloes or lightly regarded as minor motoring offences are today. And the evidence everywhere makes it certain that by the great majority the church courts on this point at any rate were feared. To be hauled before them meant serious damage to credit and reputation.

Everyone's private life was closely supervised: in those close-knit little communities few secrets could be hid and most desires were known. It all came out in the church courts and if the clerk was not too pressed for time he wrote down the facts.

These Stratford records do not abound in the lecherous detail often found elsewhere. But we have evidence in plenty – and much of it concerning leading people in the place, some of them relatives and friends near to Shakespeare – to make us often exclaim, with the Porter in *Henry VIII*, 'Bless me, what a fry of fornication is at door'.[4]

The substantial Syche (or Suche) family were neighbours of the Hathaways at Shottery. Stephen Syche, detected 'upon suspicion of fornication committed with Joan Nybbe', confessed at the court held 9 November 1590, had to do penance in church on the following Sunday and of course to return a certificate of performance. This he failed to produce at the next court. On 9 December he made an appearance and begged to be allowed commutation. He was thereupon excused penance and directed to pay to the churchwardens a sum to be decided upon by the Judge. The court at Stratford as elsewhere was almost always ready to accommodate those who bowed to its authority by promptly answering a summons. Otherwise, it clamped down with its all-purpose sanction of excommunication.

Three members of the Burman family of Shottery, friends of the Hathaways, are charged in incontinence cases. William, son of Stephen whom we have already met, was about a year and a half younger than Shakespeare. On 10 October 1592 he was presented upon a 'public fame that he had committed adultery with Margery the wife of John Pyner'. This he denied and was ordered compurgation with six honest neighbours who had to be married people, four from the town and two from the parish. Margery Pyner appeared at the same time and had to purge with six honest women of the parish: in her case the town was not mentioned.

At the court held on the following 13 February Burman pleaded poverty. This seems strange, for the family was one of substance. However, the plea was accepted and because of this and 'other reasons moving the mind of the Judge' he was allowed to purge himself on his own oath. The same concession was granted to Mistress Pyner.

Richard Burman, a brother of William, became involved with a widow, Alice Atwood, of the family associated with Atwood's tavern in the High Street. This woman was accused of adultery with both Burman and another man, Bartholomew Parsons, of the Wood Street family, related to the Sadlers. Neither she nor Burman answered to the citation, were accordingly excommunicated, and that is the last we hear of them in this record.

Thomas Burman, yet another brother, is entered (30 August 1608) as 'detected with a certain Susanna Aynge', whose family lived at the top of Bridge Street near the *Angel Inn*. He made a clean breast of it, appeared on the first citation, confessed that he had made the girl pregnant and received the inevitable injunction to go through a white sheet penance on two successive Sundays. He asked for mitigation and the Judge allowed him to make complete satisfaction by the payment of two shillings to the poor.

In the Parish Register of baptisms under the date 5 May 1592 occurs 'John, son of Katherine Getley, a bastard'. Just over five months later, on 10 October, the mother and one William Sanford were called in the court, having been presented for fornication. Neither of them appeared and the

Judge decreed a further citation. On 13 February they were still contumacious and accordingly were excommunicated. So the record leaves them.

Katherine Getley was the daughter of the Walter Getley from whom in 1602 Shakespeare bought a cottage in Chapel Lane standing opposite to New Place.

John Sadler was cited to appear before the court in May 1606 on suspicion of incontinence with Anne Brown *alias* Watton. The woman appeared and confessed that she was pregnant by him. She was awarded a particularly severe sentence: penance in a white sheet on two successive Sundays in the church and once in the Market, that is, probably, the Rother Market, by the Cross; and she had to certify the performance on the next court day after childbirth. As so often in these cases, it was the woman who paid. John Sadler certainly had the indignity, since he ignored the first summons, of having the second citation affixed to the door of his house by the apparitor. But still he did not appear in court and the Judge, following the usual routine, formally reserved the penalty of his contumacy to the next sitting. We are left in ignorance as to the sequel, for the clerk made no further entry. It is likely that John Sadler made some sort of satisfaction privately. The Parish Register has the last word, recording the baptism on 7 June 1606 of 'Katheryn daughter to Anne Broune *als* Watton, notha'.

Judith Sadler was a daughter of Hamlet and Judith Sadler, the godparents of Shakespeare's twins who were named after them. The Sadlers lived at the corner of High Street and Sheep Street.

Judith's story is a sad one. An entry in the court acts for 28 May 1622 (she was 26 at the time) states that she was cited for incontinence, adding 'she fled', the clerk's usual note when an accused person absconded for fear of proceedings. Another entry at the same session informs us that William Smith of Bridgetown in Stratford (no relation, apparently, to the alderman of that name) was due to make his purgation on a charge that he had committed fornication with Judith Sadler. On

19 July he is noted as being excommunicated for not obeying the order. At the next court, on 3 August, the whole thing was sorted out and William Smith appeared and produced his four male compurgators as directed, but two of them 'upon consideration' declined to act. Smith had, however, thoughtfully brought into court with him three witnesses, one man and two women (note the relative strengths) and they testified that 'Judith Sadler . . . did in the house of Thomas Buck upon her knees swear and protest that the said William Smith did not ever at any time have any carnal knowledge of her body . . . and did acknowledge that she had done him great wrong in raising such a fame; and did there with tears protest that she was heartily sorry that she had done him that injury; and that one Gardiner was the true father of her child'. This evidence was accepted and the hard-done-by Smith dismissed. Nothing more is entered in the Act Book about the woman; but from the Parish Register we learn that her child had been buried on the previous 21 January: 'Judith, bastard to Judith Sadler'. Going back a few years we come upon her name again, under the date 13 April 1618: 'Robert, son of Judith Sadler, base'.

Daniel Baker was a leading man in Stratford who lived in a fine house on the east side of High Street, between the Gaol and the Walfords. He rose to be Bailiff in 1603. Baker was a pronounced Puritan and during his term of office he managed to get travelling players prohibited from playing in the Gild Hall.

This righteous man was reported to the court on 28 February 1606/7 for incontinence with Anne Ward, a spinster. He was a widower, his wife Joan having been buried 16 May 1600, as we learn from the Parish Register. He was duly cited but did not appear, and excommunication was entered against him. At the same court the woman, who was summoned at the same time, declared that Daniel Baker was the true and undoubted father of the child with which she was pregnant. At the next court, held on 21 March, she further said that Baker had promised to marry her.

She was ordered to perform a white sheet penance on some Sunday before the following Whit Sunday. There is no entry of her having carried out the order but it may be assumed that in fact she did so.

Baker on this same occasion was reported only 'for suspicion of incontinency'. He appeared on the next court day but one and admitted the prevalence of the rumour but denied that it was true. He was therefore ordered to purge himself with six of his fellow parishioners a week hence on 31 March. He failed to appear on that day and was therefore formally pronounced guilty and ordered to be cited to declare any reason why he should not be ordered to do penance. As with Anne Ward, the record is silent on the outcome.

Often it was the woman alone who suffered the public ignominy in cases of this kind. We may doubt whether Alderman Baker did penance. It is more likely that he got away with paying money by way of commutation.

However, the Parish Register leaves us with an intriguing postscript, as on 13 July 1607 an Anne Ward was married to one John Perkyns — maybe he made an honest woman of her.

The church court case which most profoundly affected Shakespeare was the one against his son-in-law Thomas Quiney (whose father Richard had been among the poet's oldest and closest friends).

In early February, 1615/6, Thomas Quiney was about to marry Shakespeare's younger daughter Judith when the rumour spread through Stratford that a woman named Margaret Wheeler was with child by Quiney. She was in fact in the last stages of pregnancy. Nevertheless, on 10 February Quiney and Judith were married in the parish church.

Just over a month later Margaret Wheeler died in giving birth to the child. The Parish Register records the burial of them both on 15 March.

The church authorities, moved probably by the increased gravity of the situation caused by the two deaths, and then only after some delay, decided that action must be taken against one guilty of a particularly noisome offence.

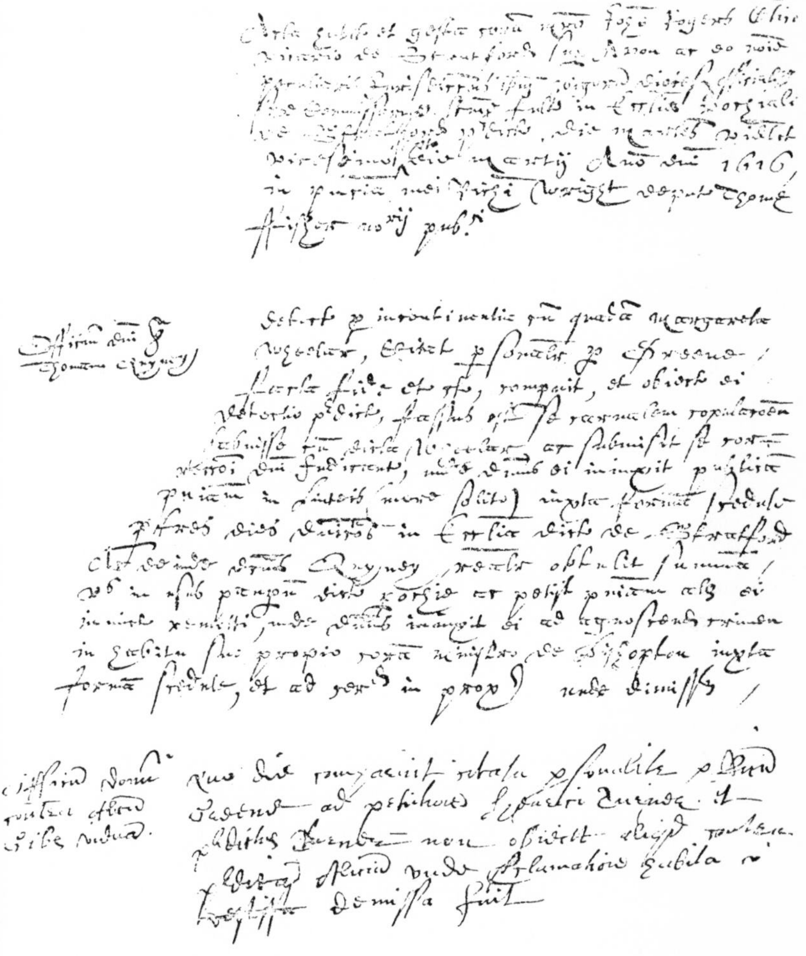

Fig. 4. THE THOMAS QUINEY CASE, 1616 (facsimile)

A citation was made out against Thomas Quiney and served on him personally by the apparitor Greene. The whole affair was the talk of the town. The most prominent people in the place were involved. It must have been the biggest scandal that Stratford had seen for years.

Quiney appeared in open court in the parish church on Tuesday, 26 March, before the Vicar, John Rogers, sitting as Judge. Quiney confessed that he had had carnal copulation with Margaret Wheeler. The court evidently regarded the offence as particularly heinous for it meted out one of the severest punishments recorded in these two Act Books. Quiney was ordered to perform public penance in a white sheet before the whole congregation during service time on three successive Sundays. He had to face the 'open shame'[5] of 'three days' penance open done'.[6] For Quiney and the Shakespeare family the humiliation was all the greater because of their social position. Society in that age was strictly graded and the higher the grade the greater the importance attached to reputation.

Quiney managed to escape the full rigour of the penalty by offering by way of commutation to give five shillings to the use of the poor. The Judge accepted this, though he directed Quiney to make acknowledgment of the crime (so it is called in the record) clad in his ordinary clothes before the minister in the comparative privacy of the chapel out at Bishopton.

For Shakespeare the whole affair must have been a terribly searing experience. Moreover, he was ill; these weeks, as it turned out, were the last of his life.

In January Shakespeare had given instructions for his will. A draft, covering three pages, was prepared by Francis Collins, an attorney of Warwick. It was ready for execution with the signatures of the testator and the witnesses. The execution, however, was deferred.

Then on or just before 25 March Shakespeare sent for Collins. Substantial changes were made in the will and a new first sheet was prepared. On 25 March Shakespeare signed the three sheets.[7] This was the very next day before Quiney appeared in court. The tremulous signatures suggest what a very ill man Shakespeare was. By 23 April he was dead.

It seems highly probable that the deep shame of the Quiney scandal and finally the shock of Quiney's being called to appear before the court had far more to do with Shakespeare's death than the traditional cause put forward for it — a fever brought on by a drinking bout, the story of which was first jotted down in the diary of a Stratford vicar two generations later.

Let us examine the evidence.

First, the story of the drinking bout.[8] This made its appearance in print in 1839 with the publication of *The Diary of John Ward*, edited by Dr. C. Severn.

John Ward was vicar of Stratford from 1662 to 1681. The note book for 1661 to 1663, covering his first years in Stratford, contain some items of hearsay about Shakespeare, including the following:

> Shakespeare, Drayton, and Ben Jonson, had a merry meeting and it seems drank too hard, for Shakespeare died of a fever there contracted . . .

This has the ring of gossip. Sir Edmund Chambers puts it, significantly, among his selection entitled 'The Shakespeare Mythos',[9] along with the story of stealing venison and rabbits at Charlecote and such like fabrications.

It is the sort of tale which, without support, would not carry much credence even at the time of Shakespeare's death. When we find that it turned up for the first time 45 years later, in the miscellaneous chatter of a newcomer to the town, it must indeed be treated with the greatest reserve.

We now turn to evidence which, I believe, takes us on to firmer ground.

A vital clue is to be found in Shakespeare's signatures to the three pages of his will. These have been minutely examined by eminent palaeographers who all agree that at the time of

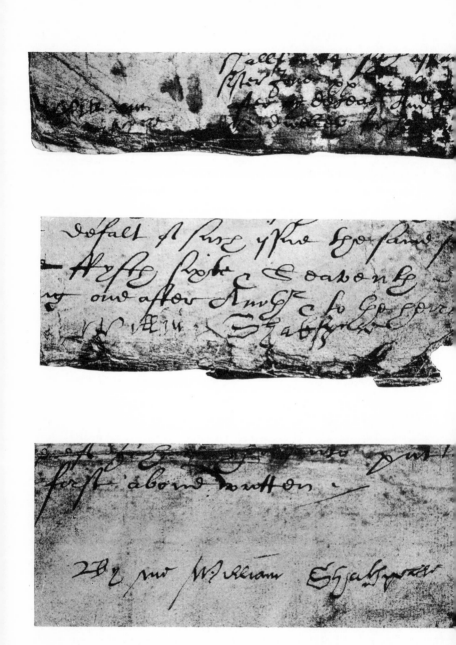

Fig. 5. SHAKESPEARE'S SIGNATURES (facsimile)

making the signatures to the will on 25 March, Shakespeare must have been in the grip of serious illness.

One of the greatest experts on the handwriting of the period, Sir Edward Maunde Thompson, Director of the British Museum, after pointing out that the will is a draft originally dated 25 January and that it was not executed until two months later, made this striking observation:

> . . . by the time of the execution something of urgent moment must have meanwhile occurred – so urgent, indeed, as to necessitate the immediate use of the draft without waiting for a fair engrossment. The draft in all its roughness, with corrections and interlineations, received the signatures of Shakespeare and the witnesses on 25 March.
>
> The only adequate reason for so sudden an execution of a will would be the dangerous illness of the testator; and the traditional account of Shakespeare's last illness is that he was seized with a fever following a carouse with his friends Drayton and Ben Jonson. But, while the poet did not expire until 23 April, nearly a month after the execution of the will, the hurried action of the business indicates that the seizure must have been very unexpected and alarming, and rather suggests that something more critical than the traditional fever had fastened on the stricken man.[10]

Ever since Maunde Thompson wrote these words 56 years ago the question of what this 'something more critical' was has remained a mystery.

Now, at last, our church court records provide an answer. May it not have been the sudden knowledge that the court had decided after all to insist on the appearance of Thomas Quiney in the full publicity of the parish church to answer for his dastardly conduct. It came as the awful culmination of the disgrace which had been hanging over the family for weeks. It would have been a bad blow for a father-in-law in full health. To a very sick man it may well have proved fatal.

This new evidence presents a formidable challenge to the hearsay scandal which for too long has marred the name of Shakespeare.

A further revision must also be made as a result of the Quiney case. The main alterations in Shakespeare's will were on the first sheet and concern his daughter Judith. Most of the biographers, including Sir Edmund Chambers, detect in these alterations evidence of 'a lack of confidence'[11] in Thomas Quiney. They suggest that he and Judith had incurred Shakespeare's displeasure by getting themselves excommunicated in the Bishop's Court at Worcester as a result of their marrying in the prohibited season of Lent. But Stratford, as a 'peculiar', claimed to be independent of the Bishop for two years out of every three. The Vicar regarded himself as fully empowered to grant any licence required and to allow the marriage to take place in his church. The Worcester sentence would have had little or no influence with Shakespeare. It is much more likely that it was the Quiney scandal which lay behind the alterations to the will.[12]

If Shakespeare did think ill of his son-in-law the sequel proved him right. Quiney turned out to be something of a ne'er-do-well, one 'given to fornications and to taverns'.[13] He was fined for allowing disorderly drinking in his vintner's shop, the *Cage* at the corner of High Street and Bridge Street; and he got into such serious financial trouble that trustees had to be appointed to act for his wife and children. Yet Thomas and Judith remained together for some 40 years. The date of his death is not known, but he was still alive in 1655. She died at the age of 77 in 1662.

———————

Edward Ingram was a son of Robert Ingram, lessee of the fishing ground beyond the weir on the Avon. He came before the court on 28 May 1622, having been presented for committing adultery with a certain Joan Clemson. He denied it and was ordered to undergo purgation. By the next court on 19 July he had not taken the necessary steps towards this, and not appearing, he was excommunicated. It seems, therefore, that after all there was no truth in the charge and that Ingram incurred excommunication as the formal consequence of disobeying the order to appear.

Several widows were presented on the strength of a 'fame' or rumour of incontinence: the result, probably, of gossip. There was, for instance, Alice Nixon, called on 19 July 1622 on a fame of incontinence with a certain George Gibbs of Haselor. She did not appear then but did so at the next court on 27 July and denied the fact while admitting the fame. To prove her innocence Mistress Nixon was directed to purge herself with four honest women 'at the next court after harvest'.

Elizabeth Whiting 'alias the White Bear' was also called on 19 July 1622 on account of a 'fame' of the same kind, though the man was not named. She appeared at once, denied the truth of the rumour and was ordered to purge herself with six honest women at the next court on 27 July. Why, one wonders, did this woman, who obeyed the court immediately, have to produce six compurgators, whereas Nixon, who prevaricated slightly, had to bring in only four. Was it because Nixon had the superior status of a widow?

The case of Margery Warner is unusual. Against her name the clerk noted 'she accused herself of adultery with Robert Willson of the *Crown*' (the inn in Fore Bridge Street, at the entrance of the chure leading through to High Street). She appeared on 22 May 1624. The clerk continued his entry: 'and in public court she confessed herself guilty of the same, and upon her oath she declareth that she did several times commit adultery with the said Robert Willson'. Warner was ordered to perform public penance in the parish church on the following Sunday, standing in the middle aisle 'upon a high mat or form with a white sheet upon her back spread, having no hat upon her head' from the beginning of Morning Prayer to the end of the sermon and then 'publickly to confess her fault, desiring the congregation to pray to God to forgive her and also to promise never to commit the like sin hereafter' and 'to stand in like manner at the Market Cross the next Thursday'. There is no further entry but bearing in mind local conditions it is almost certain that the penance was performed and certified.

As for Robert Willson, he was called on 16 July 'for incontinence', the clerk noted that he was absent, which means, probably, that he was absent from the parish; and nothing more is known of him.

On 16 July 1624 Thomas West was called for fornication with Isabella Hall who was cited at the same time. He did not appear but Isabella obeyed the citation and openly confessed that 'she had a bastard or base child by Thomas West and that he and none but he had the use of her body and was father of the base child'. The clerk, in recording the order for penance, went into detail — quoting, no doubt, from the schedule of penance itself — 'namely that the said Isabella shall repair unto the parish church of Stratford and there she is to stand upon a mat or seat in the middle aisle of the church during all the time of Morning Prayer and Sermon in white sheets hanging down from her shoulders to her feet and holding a white rod in her hand and at the end of the sermon to confess according to the schedule' (which means that she had to go into details) and to bring a certificate before the next court day. She was also ordered to pay the fees and was given only until the following Wednesday. Whether this humiliating penance was done or not we cannot be sure, for the only entries against Isabella Hall's name in the following sessions are, first, that she had not paid the fees and was to be cited afresh 'by all ways and means possible', and then that she had not certified the performance of penance and had thereby incurred excommunication. As for West, there is no record of any order for penance against him, though there must have been one. The last entry concerning him is that 'for not paying the fees', he was excommunicated; and added later, in the margin, a business-like note: 'the fees were paid'.

From the Parish Register we learn that the child had been baptised on 1 May: 'Anna, daughter of Isabella Hall, a spuria'.

The baptism of Isabella Hall herself does not appear, but she was possibly the daughter of Robert Hall, mason of Stratford, and his wife Joan. He was the son of the Robert Hall who rented the old School House at Stratford and did masonry for the town. He married Isabella Wood.[14] It was a usual practice to name children after grandparents.

The fortunes of John Davis and Elizabeth Wheeler at a crisis of their lives may be followed in lively detail. Davis was cited to the court on 7 January 1624/5 on a fame of incontinence with Wheeler. Apparently he did not appear for it is merely entered that the penalty was reserved to the next court. On the next page but one, however, the clerk notes that Davis later appeared in the Judge's house and petitioned for a marriage licence. This was granted upon the taking of an oath by Davis that he had the consent of Wheeler's parents and that there was no impediment of consanguinity. Davis was entered again for the same offence at the court of 21 January. He did not appear and the penalty was formally reserved to the next court. From the Parish Register we learn that the couple were duly married on 31 January. The court, however, was characteristically pertinacious. On the following 4 March 'John Davis, shoemaker' stood before the court 'for begetting his wife with child before marriage'. He admitted it. The Judge imposed a semi-public penance: Davis and his wife had to acknowledge their sin in church, though not in service time, before 'Mr. Bailiff, Mr. Alderman and Mr. Trapp' (the curate) 'between this day and Sunday come senight next'.

Edward and Ursula Sandles were among several cited for incontinence before marriage. The offence was generally treated with relative leniency. The couple appeared on 21 January 1624/5, the marriage, the Parish Register informs us, having taken place on the previous 28 June, and they were ordered to perform semi-public penance: the acknowledgment of their fault before the Minister, the churchwardens, the Bailiff and the Alderman.

Edward Sandles was the son of Fulke Sandles, who has gone down to history as one of the key figures in the story of William Shakespeare's marriage. It was he and John Richardson who went to Worcester on Wednesday, 28 November 1582, as sureties of Shakespeare (then aged eighteen and a half) for a licence to marry Anne Hathaway 'of Stratford in the diocese of Worcester, maiden', with only one reading of the banns instead of the usual three. They entered into a bond to indemnify the Bishop should any legal consideration arise to prevent the marriage. The day before, Tuesday, 27 November, according to an entry in the Bishop's Register, a licence was issued for the marriage of William Shakespeare to Anne Whateley 'of Temple Grafton' (a village five miles to the west of Stratford).[15]

Shakespeare was, of course, duly married to Anne Hathaway, though where and when is not on record.[16]

The Bishop's Register entry concerning the licence to marry 'Anne Whateley' has aroused endless speculation. Some contend she was Shakespeare's real love and that the bond was taken out to compel him to marry Anne Hathaway who was pregnant by him. Others contend that the name 'Whateley' is merely a clerical error for 'Hathaway'. This seems unlikely because it is followed by 'of Temple Grafton' and not 'of Stratford': unlikely, too, because the Bishop's Register is a neat fair copy written up later from notes or from files of loose documents and not on the actual day when the licence was issued.[17]

It is better to stick strictly to the records and to avoid melodrama. The simplest explanation seems to be that the entries refer to two different William Shakespeares. The surname was by no means uncommon in this part of Warwickshire; and the Christian name was one of the commonest in use then as now.[18]

REFERENCES

1   E.R.C. Brinkworth (ed.) *The Archdeacon's Court: Liber Actorum, 1584*, Oxon. Rec. Soc. vol. 24 (1946), p.227.

2   *Southwell Act Books*, 28 January 1566.

3   Christopher Hill, *Society and Puritanism in Pre-Revolutionary England* (1964), pp.322-3.

4   *Henry VIII* 5: 4: 36.

5   *2 Henry VI* 2: 4: 19.

6   *2 Henry VI* 2: 3: 11.

7   E.K. Chambers, *William Shakespeare* (1930), vol. 2, Appendix A, xxiv, 'Shakespeare's Will', pp.169-180.

8   *Ibid.*, pp.249-250.

9   *Ibid.*, Appendix C, pp.238-302.

10 E. Maunde Thompson in *Shakespeare's England* ed. Sir W. Raleigh (1926), vol. 1, p.304; see his 'Analysis of Shakespeare's Autograph Signatures', *ibid.*, pp.299-309. See also his *Shakespeare's Handwriting* (1916); and S.A. Tannenbaum, *Problems of Shakespeare's Penmanship* (1927).

11 E.K. Chambers, *op.cit.*, vol. 2, p.176.

12 This was first put forward by Hugh A. Hanley in his article 'Shakespeare's Family in Stratford Records', *The Times Literary Supplement*, 21 May 1964.

13 *The Merry Wives of Windsor*, 5: 5: 170.

14 E.K. Chambers, *op. cit.*, vol. 2, p.6.

15 The name Shakespeare is spelt Shaxpere in the Whateley entry and Shagspere in the Hathaway entry. As spelling was then phonetic this has perhaps no significance, though it is worth noting.

    At Stratford licences were sought from Worcester in one year out of every three. Otherwise they were issued at Stratford in virtue of its Peculiar jurisdiction.

16 There is no entry in the Parish Register of Stratford-upon-Avon. The Parish Register of Temple Grafton is lost.

17 I owe this important point to Dr. D.M. Barratt of the Bodleian Library.

18 For the most readily available full discussion and the documents, see E.K. Chambers, *op.cit.*, vol. 2, pp.41-52. Advocates of Anne Whateley are Ivor Brown, *Shakespeare* (1949), pp.49-71, and Anthony Burgess, *Shakespeare* (1970), pp.56-69.

HARBOURING PREGNANT WOMEN

ILLEGITIMATE CHILDREN were a charge on the parish if the father could not be found. The churchwardens therefore were urged for practical reasons as well as spiritual to keep a sharp look-out for any attempt to conceal an unmarried mother during childbirth, the offence known as harbouring. It would be difficult to bring this off in any parish, but probably especially so in Stratford, a compact jurisdiction having its own apparitor with an ear well-tuned to catch each floating rumour.

There are only three instances in these records. Joan Dutton 'a stranger abiding in the house of a certain William Russell' was noticed to be pregnant. For some reason nothing is entered against Russell; but Joan Dutton had to face the court (8 December 1590). She alleged that 'a certain Gravenor, servant of Master Gryvill of Milcote had made her pregnant'. We are here brought into touch with members of the household of the lord of the manor of Stratford, Sir Edward Greville. As far as we can see, the man Gravenor got away free, while the court made short work of the woman. Upon this allegation alone the Judge declared her 'as confessed and convicted', and she had to do open penance in the church on the following Sunday and in the Chapel (that is, the Gild Chapel in the centre of the town) on the Thursday after that.

Thomas Kyrle 'encouraged in his house a certain pregnant woman'. On 13 February 1592/3 he 'promised to withdraw the same before cognizance given to the ordinary' – a cryptic phrase which perhaps means that he was given a chance to clear the woman out while the going was good, before being formally presented. However, as he did not appear he still came under a routine excommunication. Nothing more is heard of him.

John Phellps *alias* Sutton had to answer (13 May 1608) for 'the reception of his pregnant daughter'. He petitioned the favour of the court and apparently compassion was shown, for after a formal adjournment no subsequent proceedings are recorded. A few weeks earlier, on 7 March 1607/8, the Parish Register had recorded the baptism of 'Elizabeth daughter of Anne Felps *als* Sutton, notha'.

THE CHURCH FABRIC AND GOODS

MANY CHURCHES THROUGHOUT the country in Shakespeare's time were in bad repair. Many lacked certain books ordered by the authorities and other things necessary for the due performance of divine service. There is much evidence to show that Stratford was no exception. (See also above **Churchwardens and Sidesmen**, page 24). The present records add some detail to what was already known, and help us to visualise the parish church as Shakespeare knew it.

In November 1590 the parish church was without the *Commonplaces* of Musculus and a Psalter in English. The wardens were ordered to procure them before Christmas. Apparently they did not do so for in October 1592, these books are again reported as lacking. Further, the church was then said to be without the 'Tables of the ten commandments' and 'a cover to lay on the Common Table'. These things were ordered to be provided by the following Christmas; and as we hear no more of the matter we may assume that this was done either then or fairly soon after.

The Table of the ten commandments was directed by royal order early in the reign of Elizabeth I to be set up at the east end of chancels and this meant, usually, that it was placed on the wall over the communion board. But in some places these Tables had earlier been written up on the tympanum and if so they were not usually moved to the east end. The Elizabethan order was repeated in Canon 82 of 1603.

The cover which was to lie on the common table out of service times reached to the ground on all four sides. It was very often made out of old vestments. The official order said that is was to be of 'silk, buckram or other such like'.[1] Several Elizabethan Visitation injunctions direct that churches should have a copy of the *Commonplaces* of the Swiss Protestant reformer Musculus. (It is interesting to find that among the books left to the Master of the Grammar School, John Brownsword, by the Vicar, John Bretchgirdle, in 1565, was *Musculus upon Matthew*.[2])

Of the chapel out at Bishopton, in October 1592, it was reported that 'the pulpit is not decent, nor the common table, neither their surplice' and that 'the church wall is in decay': meaning that all these things were in need of repair, or, of the surplice, merely that it wanted washing. The wardens were ordered to repair all defects before Christmas except the wall for which they were allowed until Whitsuntide. Again, the record leaves us in the dark as to the outcome. On 1 October 1595 a churchwarden, Thomas Hall, had to answer for the lack of a Book of Common Prayer with the new Calendar, a Table of the ten commandments, a 'convenient' pulpit and a 'decent' surplice. There is a brief note in November 1606 to the effect that the wardens promise 'improvement in the church' before the following Easter.

On 4 March 1624/5 Bishopton was without a surplice altogether and the wardens were ordered to get one before Easter. Surplices in those days were voluminous and costly garments.

Conditions at Luddington are revealed by the report in the court of 10 October 1592 that 'the chapel and the chapel yard be out of reparations' and that 'they want a pulpit'. The wardens were called on 1 July 1608 and the clerk notes that 'the parishioners of Luddington are appointed to make a new surplice for their minister before the next court or else to forfeit for that default 6s. 8d.'.

The surplice at this time was, of course, a controversial vestment and from its neglect Puritanism may be inferred; but too much can be made of this.

REFERENCES

1 For a general description of church furnishing and services at this time see G.W.O. Addleshaw and F. Etchells, *The Architectural Setting of Anglican Worship* (1948), Chapters 1 to 4.

2 *Minutes and Accounts . . . 1553-1620*, vol. 1, p.lvii.

CHURCH DUES AND LEVIES

WE HAVE MENTIONED before the poor state of repair of the parish church. At the Reformation the rood and the chantry chapels were abolished, many of the carvings damaged and much of the glass broken up. The chancel, as often, was the most neglected part. The Corporation in 1593 vainly petitioned Lord Burghley to exercise his good offices for its repair. In 1618 it was said to be 'ruinous' and although in this context the word must not be taken too literally in its modern sense, there is no doubt that the place where Shakespeare had only two years before been buried was in a deplorable condition. Some repairs were at last done in 1621-22, the walls were repaired and the windows glazed.[1]

A sidelight on the belated efforts towards the badly-needed repair of the parish church is provided by the case against William Smith, senior, who on 3 August 1622 had to answer 'for not paying his part of two levies for the repair of the parish church'. There is no further entry on that occasion; but on 24 October, when called again on the same count, Smith answered 'and saith that he is not able to pay the same'. The Judge promptly ordered him to discharge his debt before the next Sunday under the usual threat of excommunication. Again the record leaves us to guess the outcome; but in a matter like this, where everybody else's pocket was touched, we may surmise that Smith obeyed.

Two years later, in 1624, the court was still pressing the few delinquents for payment of church dues. On 3 September of three men called only Arthur Cawdry appeared and shortly afterwards paid. On 7 January of four cited for non-payment of dues to the chapel at Luddington, only Thomas Cawdry (*alias* Cook) was immediately amenable. At the court on

21 January he promised, through his daughter, to pay on the following Monday. The others had to be cited afresh, with what result we know not.

REFERENCE

1 Philip Styles, 'The Borough of Stratford-upon-Avon' in *The Victoria History of the County of Warwick*, vol. 3 (1945), p.271.

THE PARISH CLERKS' DUES

AT STRATFORD, as elsewhere, the parish clerks drew their pay from a variety of sources which lumped together were described as wages or stipend. Very few people could have escaped contribution to the rate levied or to the goods in kind demanded by custom. The mere handful presented in these records is evidence of that; and the cases show how persistent the court was.

The two William Balls, senior and junior, Matthew Cales, Ralph Young and Thomas Hickes were before the court on 2 December 1606 'for not paying the stipend of the parish clerk of Bishopton'. They all complied and were dismissed except Hickes and he, upon promising 'Sir Marshall, curate of Bishopton, that he would pay', also secured dismissal.

On 24 October 1622 John Pittes and John Gunne were cited for not paying the Stratford parish clerk's wages. It was noted of Pittes that 'he saith he hath it not to pay and refuseth to pay the same', whereupon he was excommunicated and so the record leaves him, though it is highly probable that in the end public opinion proved too strong for him. Gunne promised to pay before the next court. Nothing more is entered against his name at this session so it may be presumed that he paid up. However, he appeared again on 22 May 1624 on a similar charge and was firmly ordered 'that he do pay the clerk's wages and the fees of the court and to certify the performance of the same under the hands of the church-wardens before the first day of June next on pain of excommunication'. By 16 July he still had not obeyed and on that day he was ordered to be sought out 'by ways and means'. No appearance is entered but this is probably due to the negligence of the clerk in keeping his record up-to-date:

there is merely a jotting in the margin, 'he shall pay the fees at the next court'; and from that we may fairly assume that Gunne had by then paid his share of the wages.

PHYSICIANS AND SURGEONS: with a note on MIDWIVES

PHYSICIANS and surgeons and midwives were answerable to the ecclesiastical authorities for permission to practise. They had to exhibit their licences at the regular Visitations. None are mentioned for the years 1590 to 1616; but at Visitations in 1622, 1624 and 1625 there occur several names which have an especial interest.

First, on 24 May 1622, comes John Hall, son-in-law of Shakespeare and at that date the leading physician in Stratford. Like many of his contemporaries, Hall possibly studied medicine in France. He settled at Stratford in 1600 and in 1607 married Susanna, the poet's elder daughter. In the next year their only child (and Shakespeare's only grandchild during his lifetime) Elizabeth was born.[1] According to tradition they lived at Hall's Croft, a house now belonging to the Shakespeare Trust.

John Hall is described in the Act Book as 'professor of medicine'. This of course does not mean that he was a professor in the modern academic sense, but merely that he was recognised as professing or practising the art of medicine.

Hall enjoyed a large practice over a wide surrounding area. Selections from his case-book have been published. It begins in 1617, the year after Shakespeare's death, so we do not know if he was a patient. Hall was a Puritan and as churchwarden supported the vicar Thomas Wilson in fierce local squabbles.

He died in 1635 at the age of 60 and was buried in the chancel of the parish church near Shakespeare.

After the entry of Hall as a physician comes the entry of three surgeons whose names we are particularly glad to have, since they may well have been practising in Stratford during Shakespeare's lifetime. They are Isaac Hitchcox, John Nason and Edward Wilkes, each described as 'professor of surgery'.

Fig. 6. HALL'S CROFT, OLD TOWN

The reputed home of Dr. John Hall and Shakespeare's daughter Susanna when they were first married. After the death of Shakespeare they moved to the poet's home, New Place.

Knowledge of anatomy and with it skill in surgery advanced greatly in the latter half of the 16th century but officially surgeons could only operate under the direction of a physician. In fact, however, they frequently practised independently though they were allowed to treat 'outward diseases' only, such as broken limbs, wounds and skin diseases including the very common venereal disease of syphilis; and they regularly performed blood-letting and the draining of fluids. One great personal advantage the physician had over the surgeon. If he failed with a patient he collected his fee, departed and no more was said. But if a surgeon was unsuccessful he got no payment and he could be sued in the secular court.

In the Visitation of 11 May 1624 the name of one Thomas Albright is listed with the physicians and surgeons though his status is not given. Perhaps he was one of the numerous class of respectable quacks who were popularly allowed the title of doctor. The distinction between qualified and unqualified practice was then far from clear; and as the results achieved by these irregulars were often as good as those of the officially recognised, they were accepted with little demur. Or perhaps Albright was an apothecary, one of those who relied largely on the traditional knowledge of medicinal plants contained in books of herbals.

Recent research has shown that in the time of Shakespeare the proportion of doctors to the population was very close to that of today, namely one to 2,500. With the three or perhaps four practitioners we find entered here, the parish with its 3,000 inhabitants was more than well provided.[2]

Midwifery was entirely handled by women, and technically they had to be approved by the Church. But in some places it appears that few went to the trouble of getting a licence. It is noticeable that no midwives occur in these records. In any parish it was customary to call upon a few women of practical experience, the 'gossips', to be present at a birth. And in one respect at any rate we may be sure they would keep at least the substance of the midwives' oath and, as we see from examples elsewhere, they would endeavour to save the parish from expense by refusing their help until they had brow-beaten a wretched unmarried mother into disclosing the name of the father.

REFERENCES

1 For Hall see E.K. Chambers, *William Shakespeare* (1930), vol. 2, pp.4, 11.

2 For these figures and for the subject generally see F.N.L. Poynter, 'Medicine and Public Health', in *Shakespeare Survey*, No. 17 (1964).

SCHOOLMASTERS

EDUCATION was controlled by the church. Schoolmasters had to obtain licences to teach and exhibit them at the regular Visitations, or at about the time when these were held.

Several schoolmasters appear in our records. The most important is Alexander Aspinall, who was master of the Grammar School from 1582 to 1624. He lived in Chapel Quad, over the road from Shakespeare's home, New Place.

Aspinall appeared and exhibited his licence on 13 February 1608 and again on 24 May 1622. He was a Master of Arts of Balliol College, Oxford. He took a prominent part in local affairs and held several offices in the corporation. In his early 40s he married the widow of Ralph Shaw, wool merchant, and helped her in the business which she still carried on. Aspinall's magnificent nickname probably hits him off well: 'Great Philip Macedon': a man much respected for his learning, presence and ability, but possibly a shade pompous. Some think he is Holofernes, 'the schoolmaster exceeding fantastical, too-too vain, too-too vain'.[1]

It is interesting to have the names of other Stratford school-masters. In the court Acts for 10 October 1592 appears John Whyte, called to present a licence 'to teach scholars'. This was granted. There follows the order 'Let him now take out his licence from the Official'. It would cost him around 2s. 6d.

Called on the same day was Thomas Parker, but he denied that he taught boys and was dismissed. He appears again in the record of the Visitation held on 13 April 1608 but there is no entry against his name. Many years later at the Visitation on 24 May 1622 he appears with 'schoolmaster' written after his name and the entry says he exhibited his licence. We last meet him on 11 May 1624 as 'Master Thomas Parker, school-

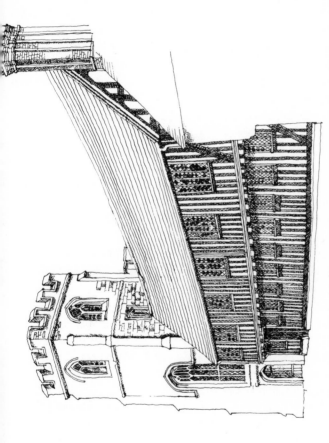

Fig. 7. THE GRAMMAR SCHOOL AND GILD CHAPEL
Shakespeare was probably educated here. Alexander Aspinall was Master from 1582 to 1624.
He appeared at the Visitation of 1624 for the renewal of his licence to teach. Penance was
occasionally performed in the Gild Chapel as well as in the Parish Church.

master'. The clerk merely notes his appearance but no doubt he duly went through the required formalities.

Richard Wright was called but did not put in an appearance at the Easter Visitation of 1608 (13 April) and the penalty of his contumacy was reserved to the next court. In all probability he later complied. He was still teaching in 1622. The entry for the Visitation held on 24 May describes him as 'Master Richard Wright, master of arts, schoolmaster' and records that he petitioned for a licence to teach and that it was granted.

'Master John Trapp, bachelor of arts, schoolmaster' appeared at the Visitations of 11 May 1624 and 3 May in the following year.

John Trapp became usher in 1622 and Master in 1624 (in which year he proceeded M.A.; he was of Christ Church, Oxford). In 1636 he was presented to the vicarage of Weston-upon-Avon, two miles from Stratford. He married in 1624, at Stratford, Mary Gibbard. Trapp wrote many works which are 'characterised by quaint humour and profound scholarship'. He was also 'one of the prime preachers of his time'.[2] He was probably a nephew of Simon Trapp who first signed the Parish Register as curate on 19 April 1624 and continued to do so until near his death. John Trapp was buried on 25 January 1641.

John Bedom 'schoolmaster, to teach boys to write' was called for the Visitation of 24 May 1622; the clerk notes his absence through illness. On 11 May 1624 he appeared, and moreover, the margin tells us, paid. Bedom was no doubt one of those specialist writing masters who were to be found in increasing numbers all over the country in Shakespeare's time and later. Some questions, suggested by our knowledge of the teaching of handwriting elsewhere, arise as to Bedom's position in Stratford. Was he a permanent master at the Grammar School; did he teach writing only after hours and/or on Saturdays; was he an itinerant master who visited the school for certain periods, or did he conduct a writing school of his own?[3]

Bedom would teach both the Gothic, 'Secretary' hand and the newer Italic hand. In practice these were often mixed, but it was the 'Secretary', the general business hand, which long held sway. It certainly did in Stratford. Shakespeare himself, as far as we can see from the specimens of his handwriting which remain, employed no other; and the clerks who wrote the church court records were scarcely affected by Italic at all until the 1620s and even then not much. At the foot of the first page of the Act Book for 1622-24 are some experiments in the writing of the Italic alphabet, using the fashionable 'clubbed' letters. But the 'sweet Roman hand' of Olivia[4] was certainly well exemplified in Stratford: Shakespeare's brother Gilbert produced a good signature, while Thomas Quiney's Italic was splendid.

John Bedom's licence was to teach boys only. Girls, apart from those of royal and noble families, were not generally taught to write. Shakespeare's daughter Susanna could just manage a poor signature; his other daughter Judith used a mark.

REFERENCES

1 *Love's Labour's Lost*: 5: 2: 531.

2 *Dictionary of National Biography.*

3 See Herbert C. Schulz 'The Teaching of Handwriting in Tudor and Stuart England', *The Huntington Library Quarterly*, vol. 6 no. 4 (August 1943).

4 *Twelfth Night*: 3: 4: 32.

WILLS AND BEQUESTS

ONLY A SMALL PROPORTION of the business to do with the proving of wills and granting of administrations is reflected in these records. A few cases of special interest may be mentioned.

Richard Horneby, blacksmith, was buried on 5 June 1606, His widow Agnes was called to the court of 2 December to prove his will. She did so, exhibited the inventory of his goods and was dismissed. The Hornebys we have met before, near neighbours and friends of Shakespeare in Henley Street, people he had known from his earliest years. The blacksmith's shop was just to the west of the Mere stream as it crossed the road and flowed by way of Rother Street and Chapel Lane to the river. Next to the blacksmith's were two cottages. Then came to Shakespeare property, including the Birthplace.

Two other people well known to Shakespeare were cited for the same court day as Mistress Horneby. They were John Nash, 'gentleman', and Dorothy his wife; they had to administer the goods of Francis Bellars. Bellars had died back in 1602, and soon afterwards one Dorothy Bellars had already appeared before the court in connection with this administration. Very probably she was his widow and had since remarried. Nash duly appeared and accepted the responsibility. John Nash and his brother Anthony were particularly close friends of Shakespeare: to each of them he left 26s. 8d. to buy a memorial ring; and his grand-daughter Elizabeth Hall was in due course to marry Anthony Nash's son Thomas.

The case of Joan Gilbie was unusual. She was called on 26 March 1616 to prove the will which it was rumoured she had burnt. After a short delay she appeared. It was formally asked if anyone had anything to say for or against her and

106

as nothing was brought forward, the judge ordered the goods to be handed over to her and she was dismissed.

John Hathaway was the executor of his father Bartholomew (whose sister was Anne, wife of Shakespeare). Bartholomew died in the plague which hit Stratford in 1624. John Hathaway appeared in court on 6 December to prove the will. By this he inherited, in the words of his father in that document, 'all that my messuage or tenement, orchard, garden and backside, with the appurtenances, in Shottery and two yardlands and a half, arable, meadow and pasture, with two closes thereunto belonging' and the residue of the property with the exception of £120, a cart and a mare and a bedstead which were to go to the younger son Edmund, and certain gifts to other members of the family.[1]

REFERENCE
1 E.I. Fripp, *Shakespeare's Haunts near Stratford*, pp.13-14.

MARRIAGE

ADRIAN HOLDER and his wife appeared before the court in May 1606 for marrying without licence or banns, but as they were able to show a licence from the Chancellor of the diocese addressed to Mr. Holder, the curate of near-by Atherstone (a relative, perhaps) they were dismissed.

Two couples, Richard and Joan Cooke, Robert and Alice Handes, appeared on 2 December 1608 for 'unlawful marriage' at Preston upon Stour, near Stratford. They admitted it and the penalty was reserved. As the Act Book ends with this session of the court we do not know the outcome. Strictly, for this offence they incurred excommunication *ipso facto*, but the court would probably treat the matter rather lightly and on payment of fees they would be absolved.

The case of Martin Wright, curate of Luddington, is interesting from several points of view. He was cited by the Judge, the Vicar, directly, for getting married to Frances Cooke without either having banns called or getting a licence instead. Although a curate of the parish, he did not appear upon the first citation and accordingly incurred excommunication (26 March 1616). However, he shortly complied and admitted both the fact itself and that the marriage had been solemnised by one William Jervis who was only a deacon. He asked the favour of the court both for himself and for others who had been present at the wedding. He secured dismissal upon payment of one shilling to the poor of Luddington.

John Drurye 'for being married out of the town of Stratford' came before the court on 16 July 1624 and brought in a certificate. But it proved to be 'erroneously made' and he was ordered to show a more clearly made one at the next sitting. Under the date 8 October is the clerk's note (probably made

before the sitting) that Drurye had to certify the solemnization of his marriage. An entry in the margin shows that he
was given extended time until the next court to do this.

Only one bigamist occurs in these records: he was Thomas
Horne, junior, detected 'for marrying two wives' (16 July
1606). He eventually appeared on 2 December, when the
penalty was formally reserved until the next session: and we
hear no more of him.

UNSPECIFIED CASES

OFTEN THE CLERK of the court entered the names of the people who had been cited but added little if anything further. There are several possible explanations of this, the most likely being that no proceedings were taken, or that the clerk made elsewhere a note sufficient to himself but failed to write it up in the act book. The omissions are tantalising but at any rate we are introduced to people in Stratford we might not otherwise have met; and the mere mention of them shows how the court affected everyone.

Richard Shakespeare, bachelor brother of the poet, appeared before the court on 1 July 1608. The charge was unspecified and it is impossible to infer what it was from the cases immediately before and after it. The clerk entered that Richard confessed and petitioned the favour of the court, 'and for the fault committed is admitted to pay before the next court 12d. to the use of the poor of Stratford'. Richard Shakespeare was born in 1574 and died in 1613.[1]

The most regrettable of the entirely blank spaces is the one left against the names of William and Joan Hart on 14 October 1608. For Joan was William Shakespeare's younger sister. She married William Hart, a hatter, and had four children. They lived in the old family house known as the Birthplace in Henley Street. Shakespeare left her in his will £20 in money, all his clothing, and directed that she should continue to live in the house for life at a nominal yearly rent of 12 pence. (The property he left to his daughter Susanna). To the three surviving sons he left £5 each. William Hart died about a week before Shakespeare in 1616. Joan lived on for another 30 years. The Hart family continued to occupy the Birthplace until 1806.[2]

Fig. 8. *SHAKESPEARE'S BIRTHPLACE, HENLEY STREET*

It was later the home of William's younger sister Joan, the wife of William Hart, a hatter, both of whom feature in these records. Their descendants continued to occupy the house until 1806.

The name of Thomas Dixon *alias* Waterman is written in the acts for 13 May 1608; against it the clerk left a blank. Dixon kept the *Swan* Inn at the bottom of Back Bridge Street, as his father Thomas had done before him. There is extant a splendidly full inventory of the contents of the inn made a few years before this court entry, in 1603. The Dixons of the *Swan* favoured the Protestant side, as the Badgers of the *Bear* opposite tended to the old faith.

Thomas Hill and his wife were cited, upon an unspecified charge, to the court held on 3 June 1608, did not appear and their case was reserved to the following court day. In the acts for 1 July however, there is no entry following the name of Thomas Hill and once again we are left in the dark. But the mention of him reminds us of a Stratford worthy in the person of his father Richard, alderman, churchwarden and woollen draper of Wood Street.

Under the date 3 June 1608 there occur also the names of Robert Perrott and his wife. Nothing more is entered, but judging from the cases of others called at the same session the Perrotts probably had to prove a will or undertake an administration. Robert Perrott was the son of William who kept the *King's House* tavern in Rother Market, now part of the *White Swan Hotel* in the beautiful front room of which may be seen the great wall painting depicting scenes from the Book of Tobit. The characters are in the dress of Shakespeare's period and it all might have been going on in the street outside.

William Smart is also entered in the court acts for the same date; but again no charge or proceedings follow. He was a tailor whose trade was with the higher class. Among his customers was the lord of the manor, Sir Edward Greville.

Of Ralph Smith (a hatter of Stratford), nothing is recorded except that he was cited to the court for 10 August 1608. But he is interesting as the man with whom, some years later in 1613, Susanna, the poet's elder daughter, then married to Dr. Hall, was said by John Lane of the Alveston manor family to have been 'naught' and to have had 'the running of the reins'. Lane was cited to the Bishop's court at Worcester to answer for this slander. As he failed to appear, Susanna was cleared.[3]

Ralph Smith provides an example of the inter-connections so frequently found in these records. He was the son of Alderman John Smith, a vintner of High Street, and grandson of William Smith of Henley Street, godfather to Shakespeare.

REFERENCES

1 E.K. Chambers, *William Shakespeare* (1930), vol. 2, pp.2, 7.

2 *Ibid.*, pp.2, 4, 12, 34, 171.

3 *Ibid.*, pp.12-13.

PART IV

CALENDAR OF THE ACT BOOKS

CALENDAR OF THE ACT BOOKS[1]

THIS CALENDAR provides a precis of the Act Books.

Brief Description of the Original Manuscripts
The original manuscripts of these Act Books are in the County Record Office, Maidstone, Kent. They form part of the Sackville of Knole Manuscripts deposited there by Lord Sackville.

The first Act Book covers the years 1590 to 1608 (with gaps) and one session of the year 1616. There is a detailed discussion of the periods covered on pages 32-3. Its reference is U 269, Q 22. It consists of 74 pages, no binding extant, in two loose sections, pages 1 to 8 being 8 inches by 12 inches and the remaining pages 7 inches by 11 inches.

The second Act Book covers the years 1622 and 1624 (with a note of a visitation in May 1625). Its reference is U 269, Q 24. It consists of 70 pages, no binding extant, 7½ inches by 12 inches.

Arrangement of the Act Books
In the original the clerk headed each Court Session with a formal statement of the day when and the place where it was held; the name and style of the Judge; the name of the notary public or his deputy. Occasionally some of these details, except the date, were omitted.

The clerk arranged to have, on an average, four cases to a page, leaving a wide margin on the left for notes for subsequent reference. He made his entries for each case in the following order:

    1 The name of the accused;
    2 The nature of the offence for which the accused was
        presented or reported;

117

     3 The various stages in the process of the case, often
          quoting the actual words used in reply or evidence;
     4 The Judge's ruling or sentence;
     5 Occasionally the amount of fees owing or received.

The more formal parts were in Latin, usually highly abbreviated. The informal parts were in English.

The margin was used for brief notes on the results of cases.

The CALENDAR follows the order of the clerk's entries as given above. The main stages of each case are given. Each stage is marked by a colon. All personal and place names are included. Everything in English is given in full and in the original spelling, though the capitals and punctuation are modern. Interpolated matter is within square brackets, with editorial comment in italics. Confirmatory or relevant entries from the Parish Registers are given in footnotes.

In order to follow through the course of any particular case the use of the Index is recommended.

It is necessary to remember that the clerk of the Court was not writing for posterity but strictly for the use of his office; that he was a man often in a hurry, his main concern being to get down what was essential for reference: that he did not aim at a technically complete record of each case: and that consequently he sometimes omitted stages of procedure and left them to be inferred:[2] or his note might be so cryptic as to pose a problem of interpretation.

Dating

At the time of these Act Books the year was normally reckoned in England to begin on 25 March. In the original records there is therefore an apparent discrepancy of a year in all dates between 1 January and 24 March inclusive. Thus, for example, the day after 31 December 1601 was 1 January 1601, and the next 24 March was still 1601 and was followed by 25 March 1602. To avoid possible confusion with dates in this part of the year both old and new style years are shown, i.e. with the above examples, they would read 1 January 1601/2 and 24 March 1601/2.

REFERENCES

1 A full edition is being prepared by the present writer for eventual publication.

2 For instance, certificates of performance might be submitted out of court. They would be filed but might not be recorded in the Acts. No entry against the name of an accused person may imply a routine excommunication.

ACT BOOK : 1590-1616

Page 1 [November 1590]

William Flewellyn: for not attending his parish church: admonished to attend: also 'for that he useth to [open] shopp windowes on the Sabothe day': admonished to desist from the same fault.

Richard Harrynton: for the same.
Margin the entry to stand.

Elizabeth Burman, wife of Stephen Burman: for the same: Stephen Burman promised that his wife will attend the church within three weeks and receive the communion at the next celebration.

Giles Rynishe: upon suspicion of fornication.
[*The right side of the page is torn and one entry at the top is obliterated.*]

[Page 2 *blank*]

Page 3

ACTS in the parish church of Stratford upon Avon on Monday, 9 November 1590 before John Bramhall, Vicar, in the presence of George Greene, notary public, registrar.

Nicholas Tybbottes, Richard Horneley, 'Avarius' Edwardes, John Barbor, churchwardens: 'they want the booke of Musculus, his Common-places, and the Psalter in Englishe': Horneley, Edwardes and Barbor admonished to 'amend' the books before Christmas: Tybbottes did not appear: to be cited by ways and means. The Judge then bound Horneley by oath that henceforth on each Sunday and festival day and especially before the next session 'that the said Horneley with his fellowe churchwarden assisted with the constable or some [other] in Stratford aforesaid shall everye Sabothe daye and [festival] daye in tyme of divine service or sermon goe throughe [the parish] of Stratford aforesaid and vewe and see what manner of [persons] are in anye alehouses or innes or other suspected places [there] in gaminge or typlinge, or otherwyse, and to presente the names as well of the howseholders as of the offenderes, att the next courte': and

120

similarly he bound Edwardes and Barbor 'that they doe diligentlye vewe and see whatt persones doe use to bowle or playe att anye other games att tymes aforesaid and to presente the same': which oaths the churchwardens took.

Stephen Syche of Shottery: upon suspicion of fornication with Joan Nybbe: he appeared: admitted: to perform penance in the church on the Sunday following according to the schedule: and to certify on the next court day.
[*The right side of the page is torn.*]

Page 4

Thomas Brydges and his wife: for marriage without banns called or licence obtained: Philip Greene, father of the woman appeared and said the marriage was with his consent and that of the parents of Thomas Brydges: dismissed.

William Llewellyn: for not attending the parish church 'and also for that he kepethe open his shop wyndowes in tyme of divine service': he appeared: admonished to desist from the same fault and to frequent the church.

Richard Harryngton: for not attending the parish church: continued to the next court.

Elizabeth Burman wife of Stephen Burman: for the same: Stephen Burman appeared: *no further entry.*

[Page 5 *blank*]

Page 6

Tuesday, 8 December 1590 in the parish church of Stratford, before John Bramhall, Vicar.

Nicholas Tybbottes, one of the stewards, Richard Hornebey, 'Avarius' Edwards and John Barbor: they appeared: afterwards Edwardes and Barbor were admonished not to present before retiring from office.

Henry Rogers: for not attending the church: because he lies hidden, ordered to be cited by ways and means for the next court.

Thomas Haman: 'for openinge his shopp windowes on Sabothe and holye dayes in tyme of divine service and sermon tyme': to be cited by ways and means: he appeared: admitted: ordered to desist from the fault on pain of excommunication.

Richard Heathe alias Swanne: for the same: he denied: ordered to purge himself with 4 others: because he put forth scandalous words in the court 'in sainge to the Judge you have bene the cause to part me and my wyfe asounder': excommunicated.

John Pyttes: for the same: he did not appear.

William Hickoxe: for the same: admonished to desist from the fault on pain of excommunication.

David Jones: for the same: he appeared: admonished as the others.

Anthony Wooston: for the same: admonished as the others.

William Trowte: for the same: admonished as the others.

Page 7

Richard Jones: suspected of fornication with Isabella Somner: he did not appear: excommunicated.

Isabella Somner: to purge herself with 6 others: she appeared: did not introduce compurgators: pronounced as convicted: to perform penance in the church of Stratford on Sunday next clad in a sheet.

Robert Gryffyn: suspected of fornication: to purge himself with 4 others: he appeared: did not introduce compurgators: pronounced as convicted: to perform penance in the church of Stratford on Sunday next clad in a sheet as in the schedule.

Giles Rynishe: for 'a myslyvinge persone': he did not appear: excommunicated.

The stewards of Luddington, Francis Cooke and Thomas Symmons: they did not appear: excommunicated.

Stephen Syche: to certify performance of penance: petitioned commutation for a certain sum of money: ordered to pay a certain sum, to be taxed by the Judge.

Henry Jewse: for the same: he did not appear: excommunicated.

Page 8

Joan Tawnte: she appeared: it was objected to her 'that she useth not to staye in the churche [in] service tyme and sermon tyme': she admitted 'that she att hir goinge oute of the churche with beckininge with hir fynger and laughinge, also for sweringe by the name of God': ordered 'that apon the nexte sabothe daye she acknowledge her said fault in the parishe churche of Stratford in the face of the church [in] hir accustomed clothine' on pain of excommunication.

Hugh Pyggen: admonished as with the other vestrymen on pain of excommunication.

Joan Dutton, a stranger abiding in the house of William Russell: she was pregnant: she appeared and alleged that a certain Gravenor, servant of Master Greville of Milcote had made her pregnant: to perform penance in the church of Stratford on Thursday next in the time of sermon, clad in a sheet and to certify before the next court.

[*Pages 9 to 14 blank, and no record of courts between December 1590 and October 1592*]

Page 15

ACTS in the parish church of Stratford on Tuesday 10 October [1592][1] before John Bramhall, Vicar, in the presence of George Green, notary public, scribe of the acts.

William Wylitt and John Smythe, churchwardens of Stratford: 'they want the tables of the tenne commaundmentes, and Musculus commenplaces, a Psalter, and a cover to laye on the common Table. And they levye not the xijd. of suche as absente themselfs from the churche accordinge to the statute': they appeared: ordered to provide the things lacking before Christmas next and to certify at the Court following: and ordered to collect the 12d. according to the statute and to certify the collection on pain of excommunication.

Abraham Sturley and Arthur Boyes, churchwardens for the preceding year: for detaining from the church 12d. given in the will of Arthur Newell.

William Smythe: 'for opening theire shopps for sale of wares on the Saboathe dayes and holye dayes'.

Page 16

Francis Smythe, junior, mercer: for the same: he appeared in the house of Master Bramhall: admonished to desist from the same fault until evening prayer on Sundays and holy days are finished, unless from necessity, and to certify at the next court under the hands of the churchwardens or the sworn of the parish.

Thomas Jones, butcher: for the same: he appeared: admitted: ordered to desist from the same fault and admonished 'that he doe not sell nor kyll anye wares after the fyrste peale to divine service untill an hower after eveninge prayer apon the Sondayes or holie dayes': to certify at the next court.

William Perrye: for the same: he appeared: admonished.

Henry Rogers: for the same: he appeared: admonished.

---

1 The year is omitted, but can be dated by the subsequent court session, 13 February 1592/3, and the baptism on 5 May 1592 of the bastard son of Katherine Getley, who is presented for fornication.

The wife of Gryffyn ap Robertes: for the same: she appeared: admonished.

Lewis Gylbert: for the same.

Anthony Wolson: for the same: he did not appear: excommunicated.

Ralph Lorde: for the same he appeared.

William Byddle: for the same: admonished.

Page 17

William Trowte: for the same: to be cited by ways and means for the next court.

Robert Byddle, shoemaker: for the same: [excommunicated *struck through*].

Humphrey Cowper: for the same: he appeared.

Humphrey Wheler: for the same: he did not appear: excommunicated.

Thomas Weston: for the same: he appeared.

John Fysher: for the same: he appeared.

John Boyes: he appeared.

John Tomlyns, tailor: for the same: he appeared: admitted: he and his servant were admonished to desist from the same fault. Thereafter because Tomlyns behaved irreverently in court, saying to the Judge 'Whye may not I lye as well as you', he was excommunicated.

Page 18

Richard Boyes: for the same: he did not appear: excommunicated.

Hugh Pygen: for the same: he appeared.

Nicholas Jevons: for the same: he did not appear: penalty reserved to the next court.

The same Nicholas Jevons: for suspicion of adultery with Margaret Brey.

Thomas Smythe presented with John Tomkyns: he appeared: admonished as above.

Henry Cooke: for the same: admonished as above.

Arthur Boyes, junior: for the same: he appeared.

Francis Burnell: for the same: admonished as above.

Page 19

Thomas Haman: for the same: to be cited by ways and means for the next court.

John Pyttes: for the same: admonished as above.

William Addams: for the same: he appeared in the house of the Judge: admonished to desist from the same offence: to certify by his law-worthy neighbours at the next court.

Thomas Sharp: for the same: admonished as above.

John Atwood, senior: for the same: admonished as above.

John Atwood, junior: he did not appear: [excommunicated *struck through*] admonished as above.

William Tommes: for the same: admonished as above.

Edward Archer: for the same: to be cited by ways and means for the next court.

John Archer: for the same: admonished as above.

Page 20

Thomas Buck: for the same: to be cited by ways and means.

Simon Atwood: for the same: admonished as above.

Henry Tommes: for the same: admonished as above.

William Hytchcox and Hethe: to be cited by ways and means.

John Smythe: for fornication with Anne Rooke, his servant, as rumour has it: he appeared: denied: to purge himself with 6 others on the next court day.
18 December he appeared: he did not bring compurgators: ordered penance, as to which the Judge will deliberate.

Anne Rooke alias Smythe: for rumour of fornication: she did not appear: excommunicated: penalty reserved to the next court.

William Sanford: for fornication with Katherine Getley: to be cited by ways and means.

Page 21

Katherine Getley:[1] for fornication: to be cited by ways and means.

Edward Greene: 'for recettinge of evill companye and suspected persones into his house': to be cited by ways and means.

John Whood: for a public rumour 'that the said John Whood is a maker of slaunderous libells': he appeared: denied: to purge himself with 6 others on 18 December at the next court: he appeared: allowed to purge on his own oath alone: which he did: dismissed.

---

1   John son of Katherine Getley, a bastard, baptised 5 May 1592.

William Burman: for a public rumour of adultery with Margery Pyner, wife of John Pyner: he appeared: denied: to purge himself with 6 others at the next court − they were to be married people of whom 4 were to be of the town and 2 of the parish.

Page 22

Margery Pyner: for adultery with William Burman: she appeared: denied: to purge herself with 6 others on the second court day following.

Francis Ange, churchwarden of Bishopton: 'The pulpytt ys not decente, nor the common table, neither theire surpless', also, 'the churches wall ys in decay', also 'he doethe not levy the xijd. mencyond in the statute': he appeared: ordered to repair the defects, except the fencing of the churchyard, before the next court after Christmas: and the walls of the churchyard before Pentecost.
Margin 12d.

Thomas Smarte: churchwarden of Luddington: 'the chapell and the chapell yarde be out of reparacons', also 'they wante a pulppitt': to be cited by ways and means.

John Whyte, schoolmaster: to present his licence to teach scholars: he appeared: licence to teach boys granted.

Thomas Parker: to present his licence to teach: denied that he teaches boys: dismissed.

Page 23

ACTS in the parish church of Stratford before John Bramhall, 13 February, 1592/3 in the presence of George Greene, notary public.

Nicholas Jevens: for fornication with Margaret Brey: to purge himself with 6 others.
[*Whole entry struck through.*]
Margin he made satisfaction by paying the fee: dismissed.

John Smythe: for fornication with Anne Rooke alias Smythe: to see and hear the penance ordered him.
Margin Inhibited by letters of inhibition from John, Archbishop of Canterbury to the Official.

Anne Rooke: for fornication: excommunication to be published.

Page 24

William Burman: to purge himself with 6 others for adultery with Margery Pyner: he appeared: because of his poverty the Judge allowed him to purge himself by his own oath alone: dismissed.

Margery Pyner: as above.

Ralph Lorde: for encouraging in his house in time of divine prayer and sermon time certain persons eating and drinking, namely William Sampson, Hugh Rooke, John Atwood, junior, Thomas Baylies, Richard Hethe: Ralph Lorde appeared: admitted: ordered to desist from the same fault. The others except Sampson appeared and were ordered likewise: he was excommunicated.

Oliver Hiccox: for the same: he appeared: admitted: admonished as above.

Robert Johnson: for the same, and for encouraging in his house in service time people playing at cards and George Shingleton drinking.

Page 25

Thomas Kyrle: for encouraging in his house a certain pregnant woman: he did not appear: excommunicated.

Joan Bragg: for refusing to attend church: she did not appear: excommunicated.

[No record of courts between February 1592/3 and October 1595.]

Page 26

ACTS in the parish church of Stratford, 1 October 1595, before John Bramhall, Vicar, in the presence of Edward Baker, notary public, scribe of the acts.

BISHOPTON

Thomas Hall and [*blank*] churchwardens: they lack a Book of Common Prayer, with the new Calendar, a Table of the ten commandments, a pulpit, a surplice, and a churchwarden.

STRATFORD UPON AVON

Jane Hammon alias Aston: for selling meat in service time: she appeared: admitted as far as travellers are concerned: admonished to desist: dismissed.

Margaret Yonge, widow: for continually quarrelling and not attending church: cited by John Poyner: she did not appear: excommunicated. *Margin* 2s. 10d.

Page 27

William Tarver of Dodwell: to prove the will or to administer the goods of Edward Loxle and his wife: 1 October he appeared: ordered to accept or refuse within two weeks.

Elizabeth Wheeler, otherwise Rundles: for continually brawling and abusing and not attending church: 1 October she appeared and in the court itself she brawled with these words: 'Goodes woondes, a plague a God on you all, a fart of ons ars for you': excommunicated.

Roger, servant of [*blank*] Whitton, widow: for making a certain [*blank*] Tomson pregnant: to be cited by ways and means.

Robert Fisher: to prove the will of John Fisher[1] his father: cited by John Poyner: 1 October 1595 he did not appear: excommunicated.

Alice Dawke: to prove the will or administer the goods of Agnes Harrington:[2] cited by Poyner: 1 October she did not appear: excommunicated.

The churchwardens of Luddington: for not exhibiting their bill of detection: to be cited by ways and means.

Page 28

John Smyth, alias Court, and George, ostler of the 'Bear': for playing quoits in time of divine service.

[*No record of courts between October 1595 and July 1600.*]

Page 29

ACTS before Richard Bifield, Vicar, in his Visitation held on Tuesday, 8 July 1600, in the presence of Richard Stocke, vicar of Alderminster and of William Gilbert, otherwise Higges, clerk, in place of a notary public.

Schedule of Excommunication of Stephen Burman, Elizabeth Johns alias Hughes, Thomas Elton, Katherine Russell, William Hemynges, Richard Smith alias Court.
Read by Richard Bifield in the parish church on Tuesday, 8 July 1600.

Page 30

Thomas Jakeman: for using the company of Elizabeth Barber as his wife: Jakeman undertook to produce evidence of the solemnization of marriage within the four weeks following under pain of excommunication.

William Pyrry and Humphrey Alen: 'for beinge drinkinge in tyme of divine service': they did not appear: penalty reserved to the

---

1 John Fisher, buried 23 June 1595.
2 Anne Harinton, vid., buried 6 February 1594/5.

next court: Alen appeared and denied the charge: the Judge, moved by special favour, dismissed him.

Sybil Cawdry, Henry Pretty, Thomas Bragden: for not frequenting the church on Sunday to hear divine service: penalty reserved to the next court.

William Smyth, Francis Smyth, junior, Anthony Wolston, William Troute, Thomas Etton, Thomas West: 'for selling wares and opening there shoppes in tyme of divine service': they did not appear: penalty reserved.

Robert Fishe: for the same.

Richard Pynke, junior: 'for coyting [i.e. quoiting] in tyme of divine service': he did not appear: penalty reserved.

Page 31

Alice Hollis, wife of George Hollis; for speaking scandalous words against Elizabeth Maunde, calling her 'whore': she denied the accusation, whereupon the Judge ordered Edward Maunde to bring in witnesses as to the scandalous words on the next court day.

Robert Brookes: for having certain persons drinking in his house in time of divine service: he promised amendment: dismissed with a monition.

Richard Court: for not receiving the Eucharist at the last communion and not certifying as ordered at the last court: pronounced contumacious and excommunicated.

[*No record of courts between July 1600 and November 1602.*]

Page 32

VISITATION by Richard Bifield, Vicar, 25 November [1602][1] in the presence of John Marshall curate of Bishopton and of William Gibbard alias Higges, clerk, in the place of a notary public.

Churchwardens:
    Edward Hunte
    Thomas Tempigte [= Tempest]
    July Shaw
    Thomas Jackeman: he did not appear: pronounced contumacious.

---

1   The year is omitted, but can be dated by the burial on 11 October 1602 of Francis Bellers, for the administration of whose goods Dorothy Bellers applies.

Sidesmen
> John Lupton
> Francis Smythe
> John Smarte: he did not appear.

LUDDINGTON

Miles Basse: cited: did not appear: excommunicated.

John Smarte: ['othe' *struck through*].

BISHOPTON

Churchwardens:
> William Inge
> William Horne

Page 33

> Dorothy Bellers: to administer the goods of Francis Bellers:[1] she appeared: granted time to consider until 20 March.

[*Pages 34 and 35 blank and no record of courts between November 1602 and May 1606.*]

Page 36 [May 1606][2]

> Isabel Bayles, relict of Richard Bayles:[3] to prove the will of her husband: cited by Whode: she did not appear: penalty reserved until after mid-day: then she appeared and the will was proved: dismissed.
> *Margin* dismissed.

> Katherine Badsey: to prove the will of Thomas Badsey,[4] her husband: cited by Whode: she did not appear: penalty reserved until after mid-day; afterwards she appeared and letters of administration were granted: given time to the next court day to produce the inventory: dismissed.

> Adrian Holder and his wife: married without banns or licence: she was cited by the affixing of the citation: she did not appear: penalty reserved until after mid-day: then she appeared and exhibited licence from the Chancellor of this diocese and directed to Master Holder, curate of Atherston: dismissed.

---

1 Francis Bellers, buried 11 October 1602.

2 The date is missing, but can be approximately calculated by the burial on 24 April 1606 of Thomas Badsey, whose relict Isabel Badsey is applying to prove his will, and the baptism on 7 June 1606 of the illegitimate daughter of Anne Browne alias Watton, who is presented for incontinence.

3 Rich. Balis, homo., buried 20 March 1605/6.

4 Thomas Badsee, buried 24 April 1606.

Anne Browne alias Watton:[1] upon suspicion of incontinence with John
  Sadler: she appeared: admitted that she was pregnant by John Sadler:
  ordered public penance in a white sheet in the parish church on two
  Sundays, and in the market place and to certify on the next court
  day after childbirth.

Page 37

John Sadler: upon suspicion of incontinence: cited by the affixing of
  the citation on the door of his house by Whode: he did not appear:
  penalty reserved to the next court.

Margaret, wife of Thomas Raynoldes, gentleman: 'for not receaving
  at Easter last': to be cited by ways and means.
  Margin dismissed.

John Rogers and Agnes his wife: for the same: cited by Whode: they
  did not appear: excommunicated.
  Margin excommunication went forth.

John Wheeler, senior and John his son: for the same: cited by Whode.
  Margin excommunication went forth.

Page 38

Alice Elletes, his servant [i.e. John Wheeler's] for the same: cited by
  Whode: she did not appear: excommunicated.
  Margin excommunication went forth.

Sybil Cawdry, widow: for the same: penalty reserved to the next court:
  she appeared and promised to receive the sacrament before the next
  court: she did so: dismissed.

The wife of George Hollis: for the same: George Hollis appeared:
  admitted she did not receive because she was not in charity: she was
  ordered to receive the Eucharist and to certify at the next court:
  she did so: dismissed.
  Margin dismissed.

Ann Nicolls: for the same: cited by Whode: she did not appear: penalty
  reserved to the next court: she received: dismissed.
  Margin dismissed.

John Brookes and Joyce his wife: for the same: they appeared: admitted:
  ordered to receive and certify at the next court: they did so: dismissed.
  Margin dismissed.

---

1   Katheryn daughter to Anne Broune als Watton, notha, baptised 7 June 1606.

Robert Brookes: for the same: he appeared: admitted he did not receive because of dissension between him and his brother: ordered to receive the Eucharist and to certify at the next court: he did so: dismissed.
Margin dismissed.

Page 39

Margaret, wife of Edward Powell: for the same: he appeared: admitted she did not receive because of poverty: ordered to receive and certify at the next court: she did so: dismissed.
Margin dismissed.

Isabella Whitbred: for the same: similarly dealt with.

Hamlet Sadler and Judith, his wife: for the same: cited by Whode: they did not appear: penalty reserved to the next court.

Joan Nason: for the same: similarly dealt with.

Thomas Stanney and his wife: for the same: dealt with similarly.
Margin dismissed.

Edward Feild: for the same: dealt with similarly.

Susanna Shakespeere: for the same: dealt with similarly.
Margin dismissed.

Page 40

Thomas Hiccockes: to be cited by ways and means for the next court: he appeared: Master Abraham Sturley testified that agreement had been reached: dismissed.
Margin dismissed.

Paul Bartlett: 'for committing adulterie with Margaret Price': cited by Whode: he did not appear: penalty reserved to the next court.
17 July, 1606, before John Rogers, Vicar, at his house in Stratford he appeared: admitted carnal copulation with the said Price and that she had a child by him and that he maintains the child and submitted himself to the correction of the Judge: ordered penance in a white sheet in the church of Stratford: he proferred 5s. for the use of the poor of the parish and petitioned remittance of the penance: ordered to acknowledge his offence in his ordinary attire before the minister and churchwardens of Bishopton and to certify at the next court: dismissed.

Margaret Price: for the same offence: she went away.

Roger Welch: 'for suspicion of adulterie with Alice Brage': he appeared at the next court: he did so and purged himself: dismissed.
Margin dismissed.

age 41

Alice Brage: for suspicion of adultery: to be cited by ways and means for the next court.
Margin dismissed.

Thomas Horne, junior: 'for having two wives': cited by Whode: he did not appear: excommunicated.
Margin excommunication went forth.

LUDDINGTON

Edward Davies: 'for not receaving at Easter'.
Margin dismissed.

William Davies: for the same.
Margin dismissed.

age 42

Margaret Cookesey: for defaming [*blank*] Cooke: she appeared.
No further entry.

The lord continued all causes not despatched or introduced until 17 July, to be dealt with in the aforesaid church.

[*No record of courts between July and December 1606.*]

age 43

ACTS before John Rogers, Vicar, on Monday 2 December 1606, in the presence of William Higges alias Gilbard, notary substituted.

John Nash: to administer the goods of Francis Bellars: he appeared: obeyed: dismissed.
Margin dismissed.

Agnes Anger: widow: to prove the will or administer the goods of Hugh Anger,[1] her husband: she did so: dismissed.
Margin dismissed.

Agnes Sumner, widow: to prove the will or administer the goods of her husband:[2] she appeared and exhibited the inventory and petitioned administration: granted: dismissed.
Margin dismissed.

---

1   Hewgo Anger, fab. lig., buried 28 September 1606.
2   William Somner, fab. lig., buried 17 August 1606.

Page 44

Agnes Hornbye, widow: to prove the will of Richard Hornbye[1] her husband: she appeared: proved the will and exhibited the inventory: dismissed.
Margin dismissed.

John Wheeler, senior: to pay the fee of absolution: he did so: dismissed.
Margin dismissed.

Thomas Horne, junior: for having two wives and he stands excommunicated: he appeared: admitted: penalty reserved to the next court.

Hamlet Sadler: for not receiving the Eucharist: he appeared and petitioned time to cleanse his conscience: ordered a day to receive: he promised faithfully to obey: dismissed.
Margin dismissed.

Judith, wife of Hamlet: for the same: she appeared: she promised as above: dismissed.
Margin dismissed.

John Nason servant of Hamlet Sadler: for the same: he promised as above: dismissed.
Margin dismissed.

Page 45

John Rogers: to give reason why he remains excommunicate: he appeared: petitioned absolution: granted and dismissed.
Margin dismissed.

Agnes, his wife: for the same: her husband appeared: petitioned absolution and promised amendment: granted and dismissed.
Margin dismissed.

William Ange and Anthony Baylies, churchwardens of Bishopton: they appeared: promised improvement of the church before Easter: dismissed.
Margin dismissed.

William Ball, senior: for not paying the stipend of the parish clerk of Bishopton: penalty reserved to the next court.
Margin dismissed.

William Ball, junior: for the same: he afterwards paid it: dismissed.
Margin dismissed.

---

1   Richard Hornbee, fab. fer., buried 5 June 1606.

Matthew Cale: for the same: he paid it: dismissed.
Margin dismissed.

Ralph Younge: for the same: he paid it: dismissed.
Margin dismissed.

Page 46

Thomas Hickes: for the same: he promised Sir Marshall, curate of Bishopton that he would pay it: dismissed.
Margin dismissed.

The lord continued all causes not despatched or introduced until 20 December and assigned to sit then in the parish church.

Page 47

ACTS before John Rogers, Vicar, in the parish church of Stratford on Saturday, 28 February 1606/7 in the presence of John Wakers, assumed as notary public.

Bartholomew Parsons:[1] for incontinence with Alice Atwood, widow: cited by Greene: he appeared before Master John Rogers in his house in Stratford: admitted that he had carnal copulation with Atwood and had got her with child and the said child he promises to maintain: ordered public penance in a white sheet on two Sundays in the church of Stratford: then Parsons proffered 10s. for the use of the poor of the parish and petitioned the penance to be remitted: ordered to acknowledge the offence clad in his own attire before the minister and churchwardens of Bishopton: and to certify at the next court: dismissed.

Alice Atwood: for incontinence with Bartholomew Parsons and Richard Burman: cited by Greene: she did not appear: excommunicated.

Page 48

Richard Burman: for incontinence with Anne Atwood: cited by Greene: he did not appear: excommunicated.
The whole entry struck through.

Daniel Baker: for incontinence with Anne Ward: cited by Greene: he did not appear: excommunicated.
The whole entry struck through.

Anne Ward,[2] spinster: for incontinence with Daniel Baker: cited by Greene: she appeared: admitted that Master Daniel Baker is the true

---

1   Anna filia Bartholomewe Persons, basterd, baptised 5 March 1606/7.
2   John Perkyns and Anne Ward, married, 13 July 1607.

and undoubted father of the child with which she has been pregnant: penalty reserved to the next court. 21 March 1606/7 she appeared before Master Rogers: admitted and said Baker promised to marry her: ordered public penance in a white sheet in the parish church on some Sunday before Pentecost and to certify at the next court.

Ralph Lord: for selling meat on Sunday in service time: cited by Greene: he appeared: admitted: admonished not to err in the same way in future: dismissed.

Page 49

Richard Smyth alias Court, Lewis Rogers, William Ange, William Perry, Thomas Jones, John Hood and Thomas Rogers: for the same: cited by Greene: they appeared: admitted: admonished not to offend similarly in future: dismissed.

William Trout: for the same: he did not appear: penalty reserved to the next court.

John Tybbottes: for incontinence with Joan Francklyn: cited by Greene: he appeared: admitted: ordered public penance in a white sheet on the next two Sundays: he petitioned remission. 23 March 1606/7 certificate of performance introduced: dismissed.
Margin dismissed.

Page 50

Anne Wood, spinster; for incontinence with Daniel Baker: cited.

Edward Latymer: he appeared in a cause of defamation for himself against John Hastinges, Thomas Aynge, Richard Maio and Francis Cooke: afterwards he admitted that he had had carnal copulation with a certain woman: ordered to certify at the next court from the Official of the diocese of Lichfield and penalty was reserved for the next court and the penalty of the four above named: Latymer further promised to produce Francis Horneby and Elizabeth his wife to testify in the defamation cause at the next court. Latymer fled and the others were dismissed.

Saturday 21 March 1606/7, in the parish church of Stratford, before John Rogers, Vicar, in the presence of Richard Dell, notary public.

The churchwardens and parishioners: Edward Wall, one of the churchwardens and Humphrey Wheeler appeared: admonished to exhibit the bill of detection before Monday next at approximately the hour of 8 before noon: they appeared: dismissed.

Page 51

Daniel Baker: 'for suspicion of incontinency with Anne Ward': previously excommunicated for non-appearance: 23 March he appeared: denied the fact but admitted the fame: ordered to purge himself with six others, fellow parishioners, on Tuesday, 31 March. He did not appear: pronounced to have defaulted in purgation and as convicted: to be cited to show cause why penance should not be ordered.

Margery Mills: for being unlawfully pregnant.
31 March: Richard Greene attested citation: she did not appear: penalty reserved to the next court.

[*No record of courts between 31 March 1607 and April 1608*]

Page 52

VISITATION by John Rogers, Vicar, held in the parish church of Stratford on Wednesday, 13 April 1608, in the presence of Richard Lewis alias Williams, deputy of Richard Dell, notary public and scribe of the acts.

STRATFORD UPON AVON

William Higges alias Gilbert, curate: he appeared.

Churchwardens:-
William Walker:	sworn.
John Wyllmore:	sworn.
Bartholomew Hathwaye:	sworn.
Humphrey Allen:	sworn.

Sidesmen:
William Wallford:	sworn.
William Chandler:	sworn.
John Barber:	sworn.
Thomas Jackman:	absent: excommunicated.

BISHOPTON

Churchwardens:-
William Aynge, senior:	sworn.
William Horne:	excommunicated: afterwards he appeared and petitioned remission: sworn: dismissed.

LUDDINGTON

Churchwardens:
Miles Bosse:	sworn.
John Urle:	sworn.

Schoolmasters:
  Master Alexander Aspinall.
  Master Richard Wright: penalty reserved to the next court.
  Thomas Parker.

Page 53

ACTS before John Rogers, Vicar, in the parish church of Stratford on Friday, 13 May 1608 in the presence of Richard Williams, notary public.

Elizabeth Tomkyns: she appeared: admitted that she was made pregnant by a certain Richard Morrys: ordered penance in a white sheet: to certify at the next court.

Richard Morrys: for incontinence with Elizabeth Tompkyns: cited by Greene: he did not appear: excommunicated.

Agnes Phellps alias Sutton:[1] she appeared: admitted that she was made pregnant by a certain John Burrowes: ordered penance in a white sheet: to certify at the next court: she petitioned the favour of the court: penalty reserved to the next court.

Page 54

Robert Willson: for irreverence in time of divine service: cited by Greene: he did not appear: excommunicated: thereafter appeared and petitioned the favour of the court: admonished and dismissed.

Matthew Martyn: for the same: cited by Greene: he petitioned the favour of the court: admonished and dismissed.

William Baylyes: for evil rule in his house, particularly concerning incontinence: cited by Greene: he did not appear: excommunicated.

Joanna Brent: dismissed.

George Brown: for evil rule, for providing meals and receiving servants and others in time of divine service: cited by Greene: he did not appear: excommunicated.

Page 55

John Phelps alias Sutton for receiving his pregnant daughter: he petitioned the favour of the court: penalty reserved to the next court.

Alice Gryffyn alias Dyer: for using evil words to her husband, calling him a name: cited by Greene: she did not appear: excommunicated.

---

1 Elizabeth dawghter of Anne Felps als Sutton, notha, baptised 7 March 1607/8.

Francis Clarke: he appeared: petitioned the favour of the court: penalty reserved to the next court.

Edward Ward: *no entry.*

age 56

Peter Smart: *no entry.*

George Robins: *no entry.*

Henry Hymus: *no entry.*

Thomas Dyxon alias Waterman: *no entry.*

age 57

ACTS before John Rogers, Vicar, in the parish church of Stratford, on Friday, 3 June 1608, in the presence of Richard Williams, notary public.

William Smart, John Wraye, George Braye: they appeared and admitted.

Ursula, wife of William Powys, Elizabeth Freeman: they appeared and admitted: dismissed.

Judith, wife of Hamlet Sadler: she appeared.

Mary, wife of William Jenkins, Frances Gosnell, John Pyttes, junior: they did not appear: excommunicated.

John Curson, servant to George Braye: *no entry.*

George Bray: appeared: admitted.

age 58

[Nathaniel Brogden *struck through*]: did not appear [excommunicated *struck through*]: penalty reserved to the next court.

Joan, wife of John Smith alias Court: *no entry.*

John Morgan: he appeared: petitioned the favour of the court.

Thomas Burman, senior: *no entry.*

John Kerby: he appeared: petitioned the favour of the court.

George Mace and his wife: he appeared: petitioned the favour of the court: penalty reserved to the next court.

Randall Wheeler and his wife and David his son: *no entry.*

Agnes, daughter of Thomas Walsome: *no entry.*

John Boyce and his wife: he appeared: petitioned the favour of the court.

Robert Hall and his wife: he appeared: petitioned the favour of the court: penalty reserved to the next court.

Anne Kynges appeared against Robert Yoxall: she accused him alone.

Page 59

Christiana, wife of Lewis Gilbert: she did not appear: penalty reserved to the next court.

John Allway: *no entry.*

Edward Tomson: *no entry.*

Thomas Hill and his wife: Hill did not appear: penalty reserved to the next court.

John Perkes, servant to William Slatter: *no entry.*

Anne Hall, widow: *no entry.*

Robert Perrott and his wife: *no entry.*

Francis Parsons: he appeared: petitioned the favour of the court.

Richard Burman and his wife: *no entry.*

John Nashe and his wife: *no entry.*

George Rose and his wife: he appeared: petitioned the favour of the court.

Robert Yoxhall: for incontinence with Anne Kynges: cited by Greene: admitted: penalty reserved to the next court: ordered penance on the two Sundays following, in a white sheet: to certify before the next court.

Page 60

Henry Davyes and his wife: the wife appeared: penalty reserved to the next court.

Francis Cooke: *no entry.*

Lawrence Nicholes: he did not appear: penalty reserved to the next court.

Thomas Rock: *no entry.*

Anthony Mylles and his wife: they did not appear: excommunicated: afterwards they appeared: petitioned the favour of the court: ordered to receive the Sacrament before the next court.

ACTS before John Rogers, Vicar, in the parish church of Stratford, on Friday, 1 July 1608 in the presence of Richàrd Wylliams, notary public.

Richard Whytinge: cited by Greene: he did not appear: penalty reserved to the next court.

Ralph Burnell: he appeared: admitted, 'and for default in this behallf he is admytted to paye xiid. to the poore of Stratford by or before the next court daye'.

Richard Shakespere: the said Shaxpeare appeared: admitted: petitioned the favour of the court: 'And for the fallt comytted ys admyttyd to paye before the next Court xijd. to the use of the poore of Stratford'.

Richard Kelly: similarly.

Page 61

Thomas Hill: *no entry.*

John Ingram: he appeared by his father: admitted: petitioned the favour of the court.

George Mace and his wife: cited by Greene: he did not appear: penalty reserved to the next court.

Joan, formerly wife of Edmund Cowper:[1] Joan administratrix of the goods of Edmund Cowper appeared: she exhibited the inventory to the sum of 70l. 15s. 5d.: the court made a reckoning: dismissed.

Anne Aynger, widow: cited by Greene: she did not appear: penalty reserved to the next court.

Anne, wife of Richard Cowell:[2] Anne administratrix of the goods of John Burdett,[3] formerly husband of Anne: she exhibited the inventory to the sum of 4l. 3s. 10d.: the court made a reckoning: dismissed.

Page 62

Dorothy Nashe, wife of John Nashe: cited by Greene: she did not appear: penalty reserved to the next court.

Robert Willson: *no entry.*

Richard Smyth: dismissed.

The churchwardens of Luddington: 'the parishioners of Luddington are appointed to make a new surplus for theyre mynister before the

1 Edwardus [*sic*] Cowper, buried 7 May 1606.

2 Richard Cowell and Anne Burdett, married 23 November 1607.

3 Johannes Burdett, buried 14 November 1606.

next Court or elce to forffeyt for that defallt vjs. viijd.' and to certify before the next court.

Page 63

ACTS before John Rogers, Vicar, in the parish church of Stratford, on Wednesday, 10 August 1608, in the presence of Richard Williams, notary public.

Lewis Davyes: cited by Greene: he did not appear: penalty reserved to the next court.

William Davyes: *no entry.*

Thomas Hunt, curate: *no entry.*

Isabel Bayles: for defamation of Matthew Bayles and Joan, his wife: cited by Greene: she appeared: admitted defaming them, saying Matthew is a cuckold and Joan an adulteress: ordered to acknowledge the fault on the following Sunday and to certify before the next court: afterwards she petitioned the favour of the court and made satisfaction to them in public court: dismissed.

Page 64

Ralph Smith: cited by Greene.

Robert Wyllson: *no entry.*

Margaret Nybb: dismissed.

William Aynge, senior, and William Horne of Bishopton: *no entry.*

John Smart: *no entry.*

Page 65

ACTS before John Rogers, Vicar, in the parish church of Stratford, on Tuesday, 30 August 1608, in the presence of Richard Williams, notary public.

Thomas Burman: cited by Greene: he appeared: admitted he had made Susanna Aynge[1] pregnant: ordered penance on the two Sundays following in a white sheet and to certify before the next court: thereafter he petitioned remission of the penance: ordered to give 10s. to the use of the poor of Stratford: he faithfully promised to do so; dismissed.

Thomas Aynge and Elizabeth his wife: he was detected for incontinence with Elizabeth Horne: cited by Greene: he did not appear: excommunicated.

---

1 Mary dawghter to Susanna Ange, notha, baptised 2 September 1608.

[*See below for the next court in sequence, 14 October 1608. The fact that these Acts of 1616, which follow, appear in the middle of Acts for 1608 is probably due to the later use of pages originally left blank.*]

age 66

ACTS before John Rogers, Vicar, in the parish church of Stratford on Thursday, 26 March 1616, in the presence of Richard Wright, deputy of Thomas Fisher, notary public.

Thomas Quyney: for incontinence with a certain Margaret Wheeler: [1] cited by Greene: he appeared: admitted that he had had carnal copulation with Wheeler: submitted himself to the correction of the Judge: ordered public penance in a white sheet on three Sundays in the church of Stratford: thereafter he proffered 5s. for the use of the poor of the parish and petitioned the penance to be remitted: ordered to acknowledge the fault in his own attire before the minister of Bishopton according to the schedule: to certify before the next court: dismissed.

Alice Gibes; widow: cited by Greene at the petition of Henry Turner: she appeared: Turner did not bring anything against Alice: dismissed.

Master Wright, curate of Luddington: for marrying without banns or licence: cited by letter *ex-officio*: he did not appear: excommunicated: thereafter he appeared: admitted marrying Frances Cooke, the marriage being performed by William Jervis, deacon: petitioned the favour of the court: ordered to give a shilling to the use of the poor of Luddington: dismissed.

age 67

Joan Gilbie: to prove the will which it was supposed she had burnt: cited by Greene: she did not appear: excommunicated: thereafter she appeared: proclamation was made for anyone able to say anything for or against her: none objected against her: the goods were ordered to be handed over to her; on her petition, dismissed.

[*See page 142 for the previous court in sequence, 30 August 1608.*]

age 68

ACTS before John Rogers, Vicar, in the parish church of Stratford, on Friday, 14 October 1608, in the presence of Richard Wylliams, notary public.

---

1   Margret Wheelar and her Child, buried 15 March 1615/6.

John Gybbes, gentleman: 'for labouringe on S^{ct} Bartholomewes daye with his teame contrary to the canons': cited by Greene: he appeared: admitted: ordered to give 2d. to the use of the poor of the parish: dismissed.

Richard Gibbes: for the same: dismissed.

Lewis Hiccox: for the same: dismissed.

Alice, wife of William Parker: for abuse of Elizabeth Bromley: cited by Greene: she did not appear: excommunicated: thereafter she appeared: by the testimony of Susan Dart and Elenor Samon she was pronounced guilty: ordered to acknowledge the fault on the Sunday following in time of divine service in the parish church: to certify before the next court.

Page 69

Susan Dart and Eleanor Samon: *no entry.*

Joan, wife of John Tayler: for abuse of James Parker: thereafter they agreed: dismissed.

William Hart and his wife: *no entry.*

Anthony Barsby and his wife: *no entry.*

Page 70

Robert Dart: *no entry.*

Thomas Watson: *no entry.*

Mary, wife of William Jenkins: *no entry.*

Richard Jones: 'for laboringe at his occupacon on S^{ct} Mathews daye contrary to the canons': cited by Greene: he did not appear: excommunicated: thereafter he appeared: admitted: petitioned the favour of the court: dismissed.

Page 71

Thomas Burman, junior: 'for laboringe with his teame on Bartholomew daye contrary to the canons': cited by Greene: he did not appear: penalty reserved to the next court.

John Pace: *no entry.*

Stephen Burman: as for Thomas Burman, junior.

Thomas Burman, senior: similarly.

Page 72

Anthony Nash, gentleman: 'for laboringe on S^ct Bartholomews daye
with his teame contrary to the canons': he was cited by Greene: he
appeared: admitted: petitioned the favour of the court: ordered to
give 2d. to the use of the poor of the parish: dismissed.

Peter Rouswell: for the same: dismissed.

Robert Monmouth: for the same: dismissed.

Richard Hiccoxe: for the same: dismissed.

Thomas Tempest: for breaking holy days: cited by Greene: he did not
appear: penalty reserved to the next court.

The lord continued all causes not completed until 4 November next.

Page 73

ACTS before John Rogers, Vicar, in the parish church of Stratford on
Friday, 4 November 1608, in the presence of Richard Wylliams, notary
public.

Lawrence Holmes, William Castell, Edward Graye, Arthur Coles,
Arthur Rawsonne, William Trowte, Ralph Lord: 'for drynckinge on
the Saboth daye in praier time': cited by Greene: admitted: petitioned
the favour of the court: ordered to give to the use of the poor of the
parish.

Edmund Hunt, Thomas Mylles, Thomas Raynolds, gentleman, John
Sheffielde, John Smart, Stephen Suche, Stephen Burman and Robert
Symcoxe: 'for laboringe with theire teames on S^ct Bartholomews
daye contrary to the canons': cited by Greene: they appeared:
admitted: petitioned the favour of the court: ordered to give 1d.
to the use of the poor of the parish: dismissed.
Ralph Lord and John Smart did not appear: penalty reserved to the
next court: thereafter Ralph Lord appeared: admitted: petitioned the
favour of the court: dismissed.

Page 74

Matthew Kale: he appeared: penalty reserved to the next court.

The lord continued all causes not completed until 2 December next
following.

ACTS before John Rogers, Vicar, in the parish church of Stratford
on Friday, 2 December 1608, in the presence of Richard Wylliams,
notary public.

Richard Cooke and Joan his wife, Robert Handes and Alice his wife: for unlawful marriage at Preston-on-Stour: cited by Greene: they appeared: admitted: penalty reserved to the next court and in the meantime they were excommunicated.

William Perrye: to prove the will of Katherine Perry, his mother: cited by Greene: he did not appear: excommunicated.

Thomas Hickox, Francis Cooke alias Cawdry, John Smart, Michael Smart and William Smyth: 'for working with the teames on Bartholomew daye contrary to the canons': cited by Greene: admitted: petitioned the favour of the court: ordered to give to the use of the poor of the parish: penalty reserved to the next court.

Henry Norman and Susanna his wife: penalty reserved to the next court.

The court deferred to the following 16 January.

[*No record of courts between December 1608 and 26 March 1616 (see page 143), or after that until the start of the second Act Book May 1622.*]

ACT BOOK : 1622-1624

VISITATION by Thomas Wilson, Vicar of Stratford upon Avon, held in the parish church on Tuesday, 24 May 1622, in the presence of Thomas Fisher, notary public, in place of the Registrar.

STRATFORD UPON AVON

Master George Quynie, bachelor of arts, curate: exhibited letters of orders.

Master Alexander Aspinall, schoolmaster: exhibited licence.

Master Richard Wright, master of arts, schoolmaster: petitioned licence to teach: granted.

Thomas Parker: schoolmaster: exhibited licence to teach.

John Bedom, schoolmaster, to teach boys to write: he is ill.

Churchwardens:-
 Nathaniel Dupper.
 William Smith.
 Stephen Burman.
 John Hathaway.

They were sworn. Ordered to exhibit their bill of detection by 20 May. They paid the fees.

Stewards of the Borough:-
 Richard Castle.
 Richard Tyler.

They did not appear. Penalty reserved.

Stewards of the Parish:-
 William Court.
 Clement Burman.

They were sworn. Ordered to exhibit their bill of detection.

Master John Hall, professor of medicine: he did not appear: pardoned.

Isaac Hitchcox, professor of surgery: he did not appear: pardoned.

John Nason, professor of surgery: he was approved.

Edward Wilkes, professor of surgery: let him be cited for the next court.

Page 3

LUDDINGTON

Master Francis Smith, bachelor of arts, curate: he appeared.

Churchwarden: Thomas Barber.

Steward: Miles Bosse.

They were sworn: ordered to exhibit their bill of detection by 20 May.

BISHOPTON

Master Richard Holder, curate: he appeared.

Churchwarden: Simon Horne.

Steward: Thomas Aynge.

Aynge was sworn. Horne did not appear: reserved to Thursday next: afterwards he appeared and was sworn.

Isabel Stanley: of Shottery, single woman. William Bevis, Elizabeth Bevis alias Stanley: administration granted. 'Elizabeth sister to Isabel.'

Page 4

ACTS before Thomas Wilson, Vicar, in the parish church on Tuesday, 28 May 1622, in the presence of Thomas Fisher, notary public and scribe of the acts.

Anne Burman of Shottery, wife of Richard Burman: to give reason why she stands under the sentence of aggravated excommunication: let her be cited.

George Badger and Alice his wife: for the same: let them be cited.

George Browne, senior: for the same: let him be cited.

William Bromlye: for the same.

George Brown, junior, and Joan Browne his sister: for not attending the church and for not receiving the sacrament.

Eleanor Badger, daughter of George Badger, for the same.

Page 5

William Davis: for fishing on the Sabbath day: 19 May, pardoned with monition.

John Gibbins: for the same: let him be cited anew for the next court: pardoned.

Thomas Kymble: for profaning the Sabbath day: 'in durance at Warrwick jayle'.

William Buck alias Smith: for the same: cited by Coates: he did not appear: excommunicated: pardoned.

Vincent Byddle: for the same: he admitted and promised that in the future he would desist from the like fault.

Richard Toovie, weaver: for the same: he denied: ordered 'that he bring a certifcat from the churchwardens,' on pain of excommunication, 'that he did not play'.

Thomas Canning: for the same: admitted 'that he did play at balle on the sabaoth day, and that it was the first tyme he soe did, and doth promise that it shalbe the last' and he submitted himself to the correction of the judge.

Page 6

Elizabeth Mills:[1] for incontinence: 'for having a child unlawfully begotten': admitted 'and saith that Arthur Layton of Potters Hanly was the father of her child': 'she is enioyned to performe publick penance in a white sheet' on the next Sunday, on pain of excommunication.

Edward Samon: 'for a common swearer': let him not be cited: 'he is the hayward at Loxly'.

William Heminge: for the same: cited by Coates: he did not appear: excommunicated.

Thomas Wilkins and Margaret his wife: they did not receive the sacrament: they appeared: ordered 'that they frequent the church hereafter and that thei receive the sacrament at Whitsontyd and to certifie' on pain of excommunication.
Margin he is pardoned the fee.

Richard Baker 'shoomaker': 'for stryking in the church in tyme of sermon, vidzt., for stryking the sonne of John Rogers of Shatterlie': appeared 'and saithe that the boy was playing and keeping a noyse,

---

1   John, bastard of Elizabeth Mills, baptised 24 April 1622.

that the said Richard could not heare what the preacher sayd, and the said Richard did amonishe the boy to desist but he would not, and theruppon the said Richard did give the said boy a little tappe uppon the head', wherefore 'the Judge of the court admonshed him that from henceforth he stryke no more but yf such offence be in the church he shall complayne to the magistrate that such boyes may be whipped, and the said Richard is dismissed for this tyme'.

Page 7

Edward Rogers: 'for stryking the servaunt of William Castle, glover, in the church in sermon tyme': he appeared: admitted 'that he did swinge the boy by the eare because the said boy did fight and justle with another boy and did disturbe the congregacon': ordered as above with Richard Baker.

Thomas Loach, junior: he did not receive the sacrament: he appeared: ordered to receive and to certify before the last day of June on pain of excommunication.

Thomas Woodward: 'for keeping companie with William Bramly whoe standeth agravated, and the said Thomas hath ben heretofore admonished in court severall tymes to desist from the same': he appeared and admitted: ordered 'that uppon the next Sabaoth day he confes his falt in the tyme of divine service in the parishe church of Stratford before the whole congregacon and there to promise amendment' on pain of excommunication.

Eleanor Brockhurst: 'for fornicacon': she went away.

Joan Mathewes: for the same: she went away.

Page 8

John Allen: 'for dauncing the morris in evening prayer tyme on the feast day of Phillip and Jacob': he appeared: admitted 'and saith that he will never comitt the lyke': ordered 'that the next Sabaoth day he doe publicklie confes his fault in the church of Stratford before the whole congregacon and promise there amendment for henceforth' on pain of excommunication.

John Rickittes: for the same: cited by Coates: he did not appear: excommunicated: absolved.

William Plymmer: for the same: appeared: admitted: 'and is enioyned as above with John Allen' on pain of excommunication.

Humphrey Browne: for the same: he appeared: ordered as above with Allen.

Francis Palmer, servant to John Hobbins of Shatterlie: 'for being the Maid Marrian': not to be cited anew for the next court: pardoned.

Margaret Sargen: 'for not comming to the chattechisme': she did not appear: to be cited anew for the next court: pardoned.

Anne Brookes: for the same: 'she was mistaken by the churchwardens and therefore is dismissed.

age 9

Mary Napton: for the same: she did not appear: penalty was reserved.

Joyce Bumpas: for the same: she appeared: admitted: ordered 'that she shall come to be publickly cattechised the next Sabaoth day, and also to pay the fees of the court' on pain of excommunication: afterwards decreed to be excommunicated in writings.

Thomas Fauxe: 'for scandolous speeches and slaundering of Alice Brunt, calling her filthie whore and said that he would prove her to be a whore': he appeared: admitted 'that he called her whore but saith that it was in his passion being moved and abused by her, but denieth that he can prove her to be a whore, neither did he say soe as he affirmeth': in the meantime the lord adjourned the cause.

Elizabeth Wotton: to give reason why she stands excommunicated: excommunication was aggravated.

Judith Sadler:[1] for incontinence: she went away.

age 10

Edward Ingram: for committing adultery with a certain Joan Clemson: 'he is enioyned to take out a proclamation of purgacon before the next Sabaoth daye to be published' on pain of excommunication.

Joan Clemson: *no entry.*

William Smith of Bridgetown: 'he was enioyned to take out a proclamation': he did not appear and was excommunicated.

Michael Palmer and Jane his wife: 'he was enioyned to shew his dismission under seale from Worster for his unlawfull marriage and was enioyned his pennance heere for incontinency before marriage': he appeared: ordered 'that he shall confes his fault and his wyfe also before Mr. Bayliffe, Mr. Alderman, Mr. George Quynie and the church-wardens before Whitsontyde' and to certify: excommunicated: 'he hath brought in his certificate and is dismissed and his wife'.

---

1   Judith, bastard to Judith Sadler, baptised 19 January 1621/2.

Page 11

Jane Pole: for incontinence: she went away.

Bartholomew Varney and his wife: to certify: he did not appear: penalty reserved to next court.

William Swanne: to certify: he did so: dismissed.

William Rogers: to pay the fee of the court: cited by Coates: he did not appear: excommunicated.

John Pyncke: to pay the fee of the court.

The lord continued all causes not finished in the next court.

Page 12

ACTS before Thomas Wilson, Vicar, in the parish church on Friday 19 July 1622, in the presence of Thomas Fisher, notary public and scribe of the acts.

Elizabeth Mills: to give reason why she stands excommunicated.

Edward Samon: 'for a common swearer': he did not appear: excommunicated.

William Hemminge: for the same: he did not appear: excommunicated.

Page 13

Thomas Loach, junior: he did not receive the sacrament: 'he was at the last courte enioyned to receave and to certifie before the last of June, whereof he hath failed': excommunicated: afterwards he appeared in the house of Thomas Wilson, 27 July, and promised 'that he will receave at the next comunion': pardoned from the sentence of excommunication.

Thomas Woodward: to give reason why he did not do penance: excommunicated.

The same Thomas Woodward: 'for being in alhouses uppon the Sabaothe day in tyme of divine service and not coming to the church': excommunicated.

Page 14

John Allen: 'he was enioyned to confes his fault for dauncing the morris in tyme of divine service and to desist from the lyke offence. He hath not confessed his fault for the former and since that tyme he hath committed the lyke offence againe: he did not appear: cited by Coates: did not appear: excommunicated: afterwards he appeared 'and is enioyned that the next Sabaoth day presently after the reading of the gospell he confes his falt in the midle ile, that the congregacon may take notice of it etc. and to certifie etc.'.

William Plymmer: for the same: *no further entry*.

Humphrey Browne: for the same: pardoned.

Page 15 SHOTTERY

Thomas Page: for the same.

John Rickittes: to give reason why he remains excommunicated: excommunication to be prounounced in church the following Sunday: absolved.

John Smart, junior: 'for not cominge to be cattechised being warned therunto. He is enjoyned to come to be cattechised uppon Sunday the 28th of July', on pain of the law.

Thomas Baylyes: for the same: appeared 27 July: to be catechised on pain of excommunication and to certify 'on the morrow'.

Page 16 SHOTTERY

William Cooke: for the same: he appeared 27 July: ordered as with Smart.

Ralph Sandles: for the same: he appeared 27 July: ordered as with Smart: dismissed.
Margin 'call him to Worcester for his fees'. He paid: pardoned.

Richard Fausiker: for the same: to be cited anew for the next court.

Thomas Courte, blacksmith: 'to shew what he hath done with the last will of Anne Courte, widdow, and why he doth not prove it'.

Page 17

Thomas Faux: 'for scandalizing this courte and saiing it was the baudie courte'.

Joyce Bumpas: *no entry*.

Edward Ingram: 'to shew cause whie he dothe not take out a proclamacon as he was enioyned': excommunicated.

Joan Clemson: pardoned and dismissed.

Page 18

William Smith of Bridgetown: 'to take out his proclamcon': cited by Coates: he did not appear: excommunicated.

William Rogers: to pay the fee of the court: penalty reserved.

John Lane, gentleman: he did not receive the sacrament.

Page 19

Alice Nixon, widow: for a fame of incontinency with a certain George Gibbs of Haselor: the lord continued the cause to the next court.

Elizabeth Whitinge 'alias the White Bear': for fame of incontinency: denied: ordered to purge herself with six other honest women in this town in public court on Saturday, 27 July, on pain of excommunication.

John Lupton: 'for a common swearer, a raylor, a slaunderer and disordered person': pardoned.

Page 20

Charles Nason: 'for detayning a legacy and guift given to charitable uses by Anne Loyd deceased': he appeared and alleged 'that he hath delivered above to the towne in sattisfaccion for the same and saith that Mr. John Willmore hath received 4l. monye fyve yeares since or thereaboutes, and doth still keepe the same in his handes, and the churchwardens doe undertake to put the band in sait against Mr. Lane, but they will not except of the band in full sattisfaccion unles they can recover the monye'

Nicholas Levines alias James: 'for harbouring tiplers in his house on the Sabaoth day in tyme of divine service, he then beinge himselfe at home': cited by Coates: he did not appear: excommunicated: afterwards he appeared: admonished to desist from a similar fault: dismissed.

Page 21 STRATFORD

Christopher Knight: 'for being in alehowses on the Sabaoth day in tyme of divine service and being absent from churche': he appeared: admitted: petitioned the favour of the court: ordered to pay the fee of the court.

Thomas Ballamye: for the same: to be cited anew for the next court.

Edward Tasker, junior: for the same: he appeared: admitted: petitioned the favour of the court: dismissed with an admonition.

Elizabeth Courte: for the same.

William Bramage: for the same: pardoned.

Thomas Dyer and John Ward: for the same: they appeared: dismissed with an admonition.

The lord continued all causes not finished until 27 July.

Page 22

    27 July 1622 before Thomas Wilson, Vicar, in the presence of Thomas Fisher, notary public.

    John Rickettes and William Plainer: excommunication to be published in church on the next Sunday: absolved.
Margin 'Plainer is enioyned with Browne'.

    Humphrey Browne: to give reason why he did not do penance: appeared: ordered to do penance 'to morrow uppon a forme stoole or matt which must be sett to that purpose just before the pulpit in the midle ile, betweene the end of the last psalme and the beginning of the sermon', upon pain of excommunication.

    Thomas Page: for the same: he appeared: ordered as above with Browne.

    John Allen: cited by Coates: he did not appear: excommunicated.

Page 23

    Thomas Court, blacksmith: to give reason why he did not exhibit the will of Anne Court: he appeared: 'and sayth that he being executor hath proved the said will at Worcester within one quarter of a yeare after the decease of the sayd Anne and the same he doth affirme'.

    Alice Nixon, widow: a fame of incontinence with a certain George Gibbs of Haselor: denied: to purge herself with four others, honest women, 'at the next court after harvest', upon pain of excommunication.

Page 24

    ACTS, 3 August 1622 in the parish church, before Thomas Wilson, Vicar, in the presence of Thomas Fisher, notary public, scribe of the acts.

    Robert Wotton, blacksmith: 'for grinding of sythes on the Sabaoth day': he appeared: admitted: petitioned the favour of the court 'and saith that it was uppon necessitie that he did it, and doth promise that hereafter he will not committ the lyke offence': dismissed with monition.

    William Smith, senior: 'for not paying his parte of 2 leavies for the repaire of the parishe church'.

Page 25

    John Ricketts of Shottery: 'for not coming to be cattechised, being warned to the same': let him stand excommunicated: absolved.

Isabella Silvester of Shottery: for the same: she appeared: petitioned the favour of the court 'and is enioyned to come to be publickly cattechised uppon Sunday, the 11th of August and to certifie the same' on pain of excommunication: dismissed.
Margin 'call her to Worcester for fees'.

Alice Lyne: for the same: to be cited anew for the next court: dismissed.

William Johnsons of the Swan: for the same: excommunicated: dismissed.

William Ingram: for the same: excommunicated: pardoned.

Richard Tarver: for the same: pardoned.

John Rymell, servant to Mr. Aynge: for the same: he went away.

Thomas Brooke, servant to Mr. Arthur Cooke: for the same: he went away.

Richard Fransicar of Shottery: for the same: he appeared 'and sayth that he would have come but his master William Richardson would not suffer him, but did send him about his busines 2 Sondayes togeather': ordered as with Isabella Silvester.
Margin 'call him to Worcester for fees or his master'.

Page 26

Ralph Sandles: for the same: cited in the parish church by Mr. George Quynie: he did not appear: excommunicated: dismissed.

Thomas Woodward: 'for being in alehouses in praier tyme on the sabaoth day': cited in the church by Mr. George Quynie: he did not appear: excommunicated.

Thomas Bellamy: for the same: cited in the church by Mr. George Quinie: he did not appear: excommunicated.

Page 27

William Smith of Bridgetown: he appeared and produced his compurgators, namely Thomas Buck, [Arthur Bragden and William Harding *struck through*] and Hercules Herford, 'and he also brought into open court these parties, John Whithead, Anne Buck, the wife of Thomas Buck and Ellinor the wyfe of John Nason, baker, whoe did there testifie that the said Judith Sadler with whom the sayd Smith is accused of incontinency did in the house of Thomas Buck uppon her knees sweare and protest that the said William Smith had not ever or at any tyme any carnall knowledge of her bodie, and the said Judithe did acknowledge that she had done him great wrong by

raysing such a fame, and did there with teares protest that she was
hartily sorrie that she had done him that injurie, and that one [*blank*]
Gardiner was the true father of her child. Uppon consideracon the
said Bragden and Harding did refuse to be compurgators in his behalfe
and then he did produce Hercules Herford, Thomas Buck and John
Boyce, and the Judge did accept of them, proclamacion being first
made three times. And the said William Smith did there sweare that
he was inocent of the fact, and his compurgators did sweare that
they did verily beleeve the same and that they did thinck in theyre
consciences that the said William Smith was free from any such fact.
Wheruppon the said Smith was dismissed without farther punishment'.

Page 28

ACTS, 24 October before Thomas Wilson, Vicar, in the presence of
Thomas Fisher, notary public, scribe of the acts.

William Smith: 'for not paying his parte of a levie towards the repaire of
the church': he appeared 'and saith that he is not able to paie the
same': ordered to pay his part before the next Sunday upon pain
of excommunication.

William Rogers: 'for comitting adulterie with Ellinor Gaunt': cited by
Coates: he did not appear: excommunicated: afterwards he appeared:
absolved upon protestation of his innocence: dismissed with monition.

Page 29

John Pittes: 'for not paying the clarkes wages': appeared 'and saith
that he hath it not to paie and refuseth to paie the same':
excommunicated.

John Gunne: for the same: appeared 'and promiseth to paie the same
before the next courte'.

Thomas Woodward: to give the reason why he stands excommunicated:
he did not appear.

Thomas Bellamy: to give the reason why he stands excommunicated: to
be cited for the next court.

Page 30

Thomas Courte of Shottery: 'for a common goer out of the church in
prayer and sermon tyme': he appeared: 'and in regard he carried
himself unreverently in the court and swore by God, and beinge
admonished by the Judge yet he would not desist from the same but

did sweare by God againe', he was ordered to be excommunicated in writings: afterwards he submitted and petitioned the favour of the court: dismissed with monition.

Katherine Brookes, widow: for the same: appeared 'and saith that it was but one tyme that she did soe and promiseth to amend that default hereafter'.

Zache Tandye: for the same: cited by Coates: appeared 'and promiseth to amend that default hereafter'.

Page 31

Thomas Lock: 'for not coming to the church according to the cannon': pardoned.

Margaret Lock: 'for not coming to the cattechisme': pardoned.

Page 32

The widow Wheeler: to prove the will of her husband:[1] she appeared and she exhibited [the will] and it was proved, and she exhibited the inventory of the goods etc.

Page 33

Thomas Hornebye, blacksmith: 'for not sendinge his children and servant to be cattechised': appeared 'and he is enioyned to send them to church to be cattechised upon Sunday senight next coming'.

Simon Godwin: for the same; pardoned.

Richard Sandes: for the same: he did not appear: excommunicated.

Richard Dankes: for the same: he did not appear: excommunicated.

John Harding, musician: for the same: to be cited anew for the next court: pardoned.

Page 34

Thomas West, currier: 'for not comming to be cattechised': he appeared: 'promiseth to come upon Sunday senight next' and to certify: ordered to do so on pain of excommunication.

Richard Johnsons: for the same: he appeared 'and promiseth to come': ordered as above with West.

Robert Wheeler, glover: for the same: he appeared: ordered as above with West.

---

1 Humphredus Wheeler, shoomaker, buried 13 September 1621.

Thomas Swanne, 'shoomaker': for the same: pardoned.

David Aynge: for the same: he appeared: to be cited for the next court: pardoned.

Page 35

John Rickettes: to give the reason why he stands excommunicated: he appeared: absolved.
Margin 'certified him to Worcester for his clandestine marriadge'.

Isabella Silvester and Alice Lyner of Shottery: for the same.
Margin 'call them to Worcester for fees'.

Ralph Sandles: cited by Coates: he did not appear: excommunicated: dismissed.

Joan Yonge: 'for not coming to the church': cited and pardoned 'in regard that she hath promised to come to church as she ought to doe hereafter'.

Page 36

13 December 1622 in the parish church before Mr. Wilson in the presence of Thomas Fisher, notary public.

Ralph Sandles of Shottery: he appeared: dismissed.

Thomas Woodward, Richard Dankes, John Harding, David Aynge, Francis Jiccox, William Heminges, Vincent Bidle, Henry Mase, Richard Johnsons, Thomas Roades: excommunicated.

Harding, Aynge: pardoned.

Robert Johnsons, skinner, and Anne Croftes:[1] 'for incontinency before marriage': he appeared: admitted: ordered penance [in a sheet *struck through*] on the next Sunday.

Page 37   24 January 1622/3

He appeared before Mr. Thomas Wilson and submitted himself and petitioned the benefit of absolution. Mr. Wilson absolved him and ordered him 'that the next Sabaoth day he repaire unto the parishe church of Stratford and there stand upon a forme in his usual apparell in the middle ile just before the pulpit from the beginning of morning service untill the latter end of the sermon and the blessing be given, and to confes his fault of adultery and shew his penitency for the same, promising to lead a new lyfe hereafter and live in

---

1 Robertus Johnson and Anne Croftes, married, 13 January 1622/3.

the feare of God as a Christian out to doe, and to certifie of the same' in the next court on pain of excommunication.

Page 38

ACTS before Mr. Thomas Wilson, Vicar, in the parish church 31 January 1622/3 in the presence of Thomas Fisher, notary public and scribe of the acts.

[Thomas Woodward, Thomas Bellamie, William Heminges, Alice Gethe *struck through*], Vincent Bidle, John Pittes, John Ganne, Richard Dawkes, Francis Jiccox, [Henry *struck through*] Mace, Thomas Roades, William Smith, senior, Thomas West, currier, Robert Wheeler, Richard Ingram and Alice his wife, Marie Jurden [Isabel Wheat, *struck through*]. Excommunicated.

Woodward and Bellamy absolved 1 February 1622/3.
Margin Each paid 20d.

'Call all these to Worcester for their fees':-

Henry Mase, Thomas Roades, Thomas West, currier, Robert Wheeler, William Plymer and Thomas Page of Shottery, Isabel Silvester and Alice Lynde of Shottery.
'Thomas Page dwels now at Grafton with Mr. Brace Sheldon'.

Afterwards Hemings appeared: ordered to purge himself with six others of his honest neighbours within the parish of Stratford in the next court on pain of excommunication.

Afterwards Isabella Wheate appeared: denied: ordered to purge herself with six others in the next court.

Page 39

Oliver Sandles: 'for playinge at cardes with George Robbins, loader, and others on the Sabaoth day in the tyme of eveninge prayer': he appeared: admitted: petitioned the favour of the court: ordered 'that he acknowledge his said offence [the next Sabaoth day in the parishe church, *struck through*] before the churchwardens, and to bring a certificate' on pain of excommunication.

George Robbins: for the same: he did not appear: excommunicated.

Margaret, relict of William Nason appeared and exhibited the will and inventory of the sum of 4l. 9s.: proved.

Page 40

ACTS before Mr. Thomas Wilson, in his house, 11 February 1622/3 in the presence of Thomas Fisher, notary public and scribe of the acts.

Richard Ingram: for incontinence with Alice Emottes: he appeared: admitted: ordered 'that he should acknowledge his said offence penitently before Mr. George Quynie and the churchwardens of the parish of Stratford, and to certifie the performance therof under the handes of the said Mr. Quynie and the said churchwardens before the next Sabaoth day', on pain of excommunication: absolved. *Margin* received 10s. 8d.

Page 41

Alice Emottes alias Ingram: for incontinence with Richard Ingram: she appeared in the house of Mr. Wilson: admitted: ordered to acknowledge the offence before Mr. Quynie and the churchwardens of Stratford with Ingram on pain of excommunication: absolved. *Margin* received 10s. 8d.

George Robbins alias Whittingdalle: 25 March in the house of Mr. Wilson: he appeared: petitioned absolution: absolved and dismissed with monition.

William Plymmer of Shottery: appeared: absolved.

Page 42

22 March 1622/3 in the house of Mr. Wilson.

George Locksley appeared: petitioned absolution from the sentence of excommunication for not appearing: absolved: dismissed with monition.

[*No record of courts in 1623*]

Page 43

VISITATION by Mr. Thomas Wilson, Vicar, held in the parish church on Tuesday, 11 May 1624, in the presence of Thomas Fisher, notary public in place of the Registrar.

STRATFORD

Master Simon Trap, bachelor of arts, curate: he appeared: he has not a licence in writing.

Churchwardens:-
Christopher Smith
Henry Norman
John Barber
Thomas Burnell

They appeared and were sworn: given until Saturday following to

exhibit their bill of detection.
Margin paid.

Stewards:-
  Richard Robbins
  Edward Rogers
  Roger Barnard
  John Hatheway

Robins, Rogers, Hatheway were sworn.
Barnard was not sworn and did not appear: afterwards he appeared and was sworn.

Page 44

Master John Trap, bachelor of arts, schoolmaster: he appeared.
  Margin paid.

Master John Bedom, schoolmaster, to teach writing: he appeared.
  Margin paid.

Master Thomas Parker, schoolmaster: he appeared.
  Margin paid.

Isaac Hitchcox, surgeon: he appeared.

Edward Wilkes, surgeon: he appeared.

Thomas Aylbright: he appeared.

Page 45

LUDDINGTON

Master Francis Smith, curate, bachelor of arts: he appeared.

Churchwarden:-
  William Mosely: he did not appear: penalty reserved.

Steward:-
  Myles Bosse: he appeared: sworn.

BISHOPTON

Master Richard Holder, curate: he appeared.

Churchwarden:-
  John Addams: he did not appear: penalty reserved to Saturday next.

Steward:-
  William Aynge: he appeared: sworn.

The lord judge continued all causes and admonished the churchwardens and stewards to exhibit the bills of detection before Pentecost.

Page 46

ACTS before Mr. Thomas Wilson, Vicar, in the parish church on 22 May 1624 in the presence of Thomas Fisher, notary public in place of the Registrar.

John Gunn: 'for not paying the parish clark his wages': he appeared: ordered 'that he doe paie the clarkes wages and the fees of the court, and to certifie the performance of the same under the handes of the churchwardens before the first day of June next', on pain of excommunication.

Roger Masie: for the same: cited by Strayne: he did not appear: excommunicated: afterwards he appeared: ordered 'that he pay the clark his wages and the fees of the court before the first of June'.

Thomas Horne: for the same: to be cited anew for the next court.

Richard Hewes: for the same: he paid: dismissed.

Page 47

Richard Bartlet: 'for refusing to come to be cattechised': cited by Strayne: he did not appear: to be excommunicated: ordered 'that hereafter he doe come diligentlie to be cattechised everie Sabaoth day untill he can answer the minister in the principles of the christian religion', on pain of excommunication.

William Bartlet: for the same: cited by Strayne: he did not appear: to be excommunicated: afterwards he appeared 'and the apparitor uppon his oathe hath delivered that the said William Bartlet did, when he was cited speak reproachfull and revilinge words of this court, viz., "Shyte uppon the court" ': ordered 'that uppon the next Sabaoth day he repaire to the parishe church of Stratford aforesaid in his usual apparell at the beginning of Morning Prayer and to stand from that tyme untill the sermon be ended in the midle ile, and then to confes his fault publickly before the congregacion' upon pain of excommunication 'and also to come diligently to be chattechised hereafter everie Sabaoth day until he can answer the minister in the principles of the christian religion'.

Henry Mace: for the same: he appeared: submitted himself and petitioned the favour of the court: ordered as with Richard Bartlet, upon pain of excommunication.

Page 48

Margery Warner, wife of John Warner: 'she hath accused herselfe of adulterie with Robert Wilson of the Crowne, whereuppon she hath ben cited, and now she appereth personalie, and in publick courte she confesseth herselfe guiltie of the same, and uppon her oath shee declareth that she did 2 severall tymes committ adulterie with the said Robert Wilson, whereupon the Judge of this court (for her said offence) hath enioyned her that uppon the next Sabaoth day shee repaire unto her parishe church of Stratford at the beginning of Morning Prayer, and there to stand in the midle ile uppon a highe matt or a forme with a white sheet uppon her back spred, having no hatt uppon her head, untill the sermon be ended and then and there publickly to confes her said fault, desiring the congregacion to pray to God to forgive her, and also to promise never to comitt the lyke sinne hereafter, and to certifie of the performance of the same under the hands of the minister and churchwardens before the first day of June next on pain of excommunicacion, and also she is enioyned to stand in the lyke manner at the Market Cross the next Thursday' according to the form of the schedule.

Page 49

Eleanor, wife of Thomas Silvester: 'for blaspheaming the name of God in saing that God did doate and that God knew not what he did, with manie other blasphemous speeches and cursed oathes': she appeared: admitted 'that she did speak such wordes': ordered 'that upon Sunday, the 30th of May she repaire to the parishe church at the beginning of Morning Prayer and ther to performe her pennance' on pain of excommunication.

Stephen Lea: 'for singing profane and filthie songs, scoffing and deriding on ministers and the profession of religion': he appeared: admonished hereafter to desist hereafter from the fault: which he promised to do.

Thomas Clark: 'for a drunckard': to be cited anew for the next court.

Page 50

BISHOPTON

John Adams: to be cited anew for the next court.

LUDDINGTON

Sybil Davis: to be cited anew for the next court.

The churchwardens of Stratford: *no entry*.

The lord continued all causes not finished until the next court.

Page 51

16th July 1624 before Mr. Thomas Wilson, bachelor of divinity, etc.

William Bartlett: 'for not answringe to the questions in the catechism': he was sought: to be cited by ways and means.

Henry Mace: for the same: cited by Strayne: did not appear: excommunicated: penalty reserved: to be declared excommunicated after the,next Sunday.

John Gunne: 'for not paying the clark his wages': sought by Strayne: to be cited by ways and means for the next court.
Margin 'he will pay the fees at the next court'.

Reginald Massie: for the same: sought by Strayne: to be cited by ways and means.
Margin He satisfied the churchwarden. He promised the fees at the next court.

Stephen Lea: 'for singing of profane songs': cited by Strayne: he did not appear: excommunicated: afterwards at midday he appeared: ordered penance, that 'he before Sunday come senight next to repaire to Mr. Bailie, Mr. Alderman, the churchwardens of Stratford and to procure them to come into some convenient place by Mr. Bailie to be appointed and there to confesse before them according to the forme of a schedle' and to certify.

Thomas Clarke: 'for being drunck': cited by Strayne: he did not appear: excommunicated: afterwards he appeared: denied: to purge himself with 3 others on the next court day.
Margin 'he is presented for not paying his fees': admitted: ordered as in the schedule.

Elinor Silvester: 'for blaspheming of Godes most holy name': cited by Strayne: she did not appear: excommunication revoked and again ordered 'to come before Mr. Bailie, Mr. Alderman and the minister of the towne and parish before Sunday next' on pain of excommunication.

Page 52

Robert Wilson: for incontinence: he is absent.

John Drurye: 'for being married out of the town of Stratford': he appeared and introduced a certificate erroneously made: ordered to introduce a better and more clearly made certificate in the next court.
Margin he promised to do so.

Margery Warner: 'for incontinencye with Robert Wilson': cited by Strayne: she did not appear: excommunicated.

Richard Wheeler: 'for calling the wife of Richard Brookes whore and sowlike whore, with divers other filthy speeches': he appeared: admitted [and said] 'that the wife of Richard Brookes calling him rogue, he replyed that if he were a rogue she was a whore': ordered 'to repayre unto the parish church of Stratford the next Sabaoth at Morning Prayer and there to stand during the tyme of Morning Prayer before the pulpitt in his usuall apparrell until thend of the second lesson penitently to acknowledge his fault' according to the schedule.

Katherine Shingleton, wife of Thomas Shingleton: 'for calling the widow Alderne whore and saying that all her children were bastards': cited by Strayne on Tuesday last: she did not appear: excommunicated.

Thomas West: 'for incontinencye with Isabella Hall': cited by Strayne: he did not appear: excommunicated.

Page 53

Isabella Hall:[1] for incontinence: she appeared: 'she confesseth that she had a bastard or base child by Thomas West and that he and none but he had the use of her body and was the father of the base child': ordered penance namely 'that the said Isabella shall repayre unto the parish church of Stratford and there she is to stand upon a matt or seate in the midle ile of the church during all the tyme of Morning Prayer and sermon in white sheets hanging downe from her shoulders to her feet and holding a white rod in her hand and until the end of the sermon to confesse according to a shedle and to bring a certificate' before the next court: ordered to pay the fees of the court before the following Wednesday.

Alice Clark: 'for saying that Elizabeth Raynoldes was Abraham Allway his whore': cited by Strayne: she did not appear: excommunicated: afterwards she appeared: denied: ordered to purge herself with 3 others at the next court.

Anne Lane: 'for calling of Katherine Trowt whore': cited by Strayne: she did not appear: excommunicated: afterwards she appeared: admitted 'that she called Katherine Trowt whore and she sayth moreover that William Bartlett hath publicqely confessed before witnesses that Katherine Trowt did come to bed to him': the present churchwardnes ordered to denounce him for the offence and to cite him.

Richard Johnsons: 'for not coming to be catechised': he appeared:

1   Anna filia Isabelle Hall, a spuria, baptised 1 May 1624.

ordered to appear in the church of Stratford at Evening Prayer to undergo examination on the questions of the Catechism: the fees were paid.

William Wylye: for the same: he appeared: ordered 'to prepare himself to answere to the catechisme questions upon Sunday next come fortnight' and to certify before the next court.
Margin fees owing.

Richard Bartlet: for the same: ordered as with Johnsons: did not pay fees, therefore excommunicated.

Stephen Bartlet: for the same: he appeared: ordered to prepare himself to respond to the minister in the questions of the Catechism on the Sunday week in the church of Stratford and to introduce a certificate before the next court: afterwards excommunicated because fees were not paid.

Robert Johnsons, junior: to exhibit the will of Avisia Clark.
Margin he exhibited the will.

Page 54

Thomas Swann: for not coming to be catechised: 'injoyned to come to the church of Stratford upon Sunday come senight next and to answere to the Catachisme questions' on pain of excommunication.
Margin paid.

John Addams: sworn as churchwarden of Bishopton: he promised the fees after midday.
Margin fee received.

Page 55

Friday, 3 September 1624.

William Bartlett: 'for not ansuring to the questions in the catachisame, as also presented for a fame of incontinency with Katherine Trowt': to purge himself with 4 others in the next court: the proclamation was renewed.
Margin received 8d. and 10d. for Mr. Wilson.

Katherine Trowt: 'for a fame of incontinency with William Bartlett': she did not appear: excommunicated: afterwards appeared: ordered to appear on 8 June to see William Bartlett undergo purgation.
Margin received 8d. for Mr. Wilson.

Elizabeth Burman: 'for not coming to church': she did not appear: excommunicated.
Margin excommunication.

Elinor Badger: for the same: to be cited by ways and means.

Page 56

Joan, daughter of George Browne: for the same: she did not appear: excommunicated.

Arthur Cawdrie: 'for not paying his dues to the churche. It is paid'. *Margin* 'call for the fees': received 8d. for Mr. Wilson.

Arthur Coates: for the same: he did not appear: excommunicated.

George Browne: for the same: to be cited by ways and means.

John Mase: 'for suffering drunckenes and fightinge with much other disorder in his house on the Sabaoth day in tyme of praires': ordered to confess his fault before the magistrate, churchwardnes and the minister and to pay 12d. to the use of the poor and to certify in the next court: excommunicated for not paying the fees. *Margin* received 8d. for Mr. Wilson.

Page 57

William Ball: 'for not receaving the communion at Easter nor since': ordered to receive the sacrament from the hands of the minister' on the next Sunday and to certify. *Margin* excommunication for not paying fees.

Mary Ball, wife of William: for the same: ordered as for William.

Thomas West: 'for not paying his fees': excommunicated. *Margin* the fees were paid.

Isabella Hall: for the same: to be cited by ways and means.

Roger Massie: for the same. *Margin* the fees were paid.

Thomas Clarke: for the same: excommunicated.

Page 58

Wednesday 8 October 1624.

John Durye and his wife: to certify the solemnization of matrimony on this day and to pay the fees before the next court. *Margin* at the next court.

Isabella Hall: for not certifying performance of penance: excommunicated.

The lady Frekleton: 'for a recusant in not coming to church': to be cited by ways and means.

Elinor Badger: for not coming to church: to be cited by ways and means.

George Browne: cited by Strayne: excommunicated.

Margaret Nason: 'for not paying her childrens legacies'.
  Margin 'call for the fee of apperance'.

Page 59

Richard Bartlett: to purge himself: the proclamation was renewed: cited for not paying the fees of appearance: excommunicated for refusing to pay the fees of appearance.

Stephen Bartlett: for refusing to pay the fees of appearance: excommunicated.

Katherine Trowt: let the case stand until William Bartlett purges himself.

John Hemings alias Ames: 'for a fame of incontinency with Elizabeth Court': denied: to purge himself with 6 others of his honest neighbours at the next court.

Elizabeth Court: 'for a fame of incontinency with the said Hemings': to purge herself similarly.

Page 60

Francis Norton: to prove the will of Abraham Allaway.[1]

Monday, 6 December 1624.

William Bartlett: to purge himself on this day: he appeared: introduced as compurgators Thomas Court, George Bridges, James Newell, Richard Lynes: dismissed.

Catherine Trowt: the case to stand until the purgation of William Bartlett.

Thomas Tailer and Elizabeth his wife of Bishopton: 'for recusants in not coming to the churche of Bishopton this Easter yere'.

John Hemings alias Ames: [to purge himself with six others: he appeared and introduced as compurgators Thomas Robins, Thomas Stannell, Thomas Woodward, Thomas Dyer, John Walton, John Ward: afterwards Hemings asked to purge himself on the next court day *struck through*]: he appeared: admitted the fault: petitioned the favour of the judge: the case was adjourned for consideration.

Elizabeth Court of Bishopton: [to purge herself with 6 others *struck through*]: ordered to attend the next court to see further process against Hemings.

---

1   Abraham Alloway, buried 20 September 1624.

Page 61

Francis Nortune: to prove the will of Abraham Allaway: he appeared and introduced the will.

Thomas Tibbottes: *no entry.*

Mistress Frekleton: 'for a recusant': to be cited by ways and means.
Margin citation renewed.

Lawrence Manning: *no entry.*

Richard Bartlett: he stands excommunicated for not paying the fees of appearance.

Richard Hughes: *no entry.*

John Shawe: to . . . *entry unfinished.*

Page 62

William Whellar: *no entry.*

John Hathway: to prove the will of Bartholomew Hathaway:[1] the will was introduced: dismissed.

Mr. Tiler: to prove the will of his mother: he petitioned for time to the next court to introduce his justification [or, liquidation of debt].

Elizabeth Wattane: she stands excommunicated: 'she is to appeare at one of the clock at Mr. Wilsons howse'.
Margin she owes the fee.

Stephen Lee: for not certifying performance of penance: penalty reserved to the next court.

John Swanne alias Hethe: *no entry.*

Ursula Erle: *no entry.*

Page 63

Elizabeth Richardson, relict of William Richardson:[2] to prove the will of her husband at the next court.

7 January 1624/5.

Mistress Frekleton of Stratford: 'for a recusant': to be cited by ways and means.

John Davies: 'for a fame of incontinency with Elizabeth Wheler': penalty reserved to the next court.

---

1 Bartholomew Hathaway, buried 20 October 1624.

2 William Richardson, buried 18 November 1624.

John Heminges alias Ames: he appeared: admitted: ordered 'that he should repaire to the church of Stratford uppon Sunday come senight and there is to stand befor the pulpitt in the midle ile of the church with a white sheet hanging down from his shoulders to his feete, holding a white rod in his hand and penitently to acknowledge his fault according to the forme of the schedule'.

Elizabeth Court: similarly as with Hemings: she did not appear: excommunicated.

Page 64

Elizabeth Richardson: to prove the will of her husband in the next court.

Robert Earle: in the next court.

Richard Bartlett: 'for not paying of his fees': to be cited by ways and means.

Joan Bailese: to administer the goods of her husband: to be cited by ways and means.

John Smart of Luddington: 'for not paying of his dues to the church': cited by Strayne: to be cited by ways and means.

William Smart of Luddington: for the same: to be cited by ways and means.

Thomas Cawdry alias Cook of Luddington: for the same: he promised through his daughter to pay on Monday next.

William Moseley of Luddington: for the same: admonished him to appear on the second court day from this.

Page 65

John Davies: he appeared before the Judge in the Judge's house: petitioned a marriage licence: granted upon taking of an oath by Davies that he had the consent of the girl's, Elizabeth Wheeler's, parents and that there is no consanguinity.[1]

21 January 1624/5.

The lady Frekelton: to be cited by ways and means: renewed.

John Davies: 'for a fame of incontinency with Elizabeth Wheeler': penalty reserved until the next court.

John Hemings alias Ames: to certify performance of penance: penalty reserved to the next court.

---

1   John Davis and Elizabeth Wheeler, married 31 January 1624/5.

Elizabeth Court: she stands excommunicated.

Page 66 SHOTTERY

Elizabeth Richardson: to prove the will of her husband: cited by Strayne: she did not appear: penalty reserved to the next court.

Richard Bartlett of Stratford: 'for not paying of his fees': he was cited by ways and means on Wednesday last at the Mills near Stratford: he did not appear: excommunicated.

Joan Bailisse: to administer the goods of Matthew Baylie[1] her husband: to be cited by ways and means after mid-day.

John Smart of Luddington: he was cited by ways and means: reserved to the second court day.

William Smart: reserved to the second court day.

Thomas Cawdry alias Cook: he promised to pay the fees on Monday.

Edward Sandells and Ursula his wife:[2] 'for being incontinent before marriage': he appeared: ordered to acknowledge the fault before the bailiff of Stratford, the churchwardens and the minister and the alderman, and to certify in the next court.

Page 67

Elizabeth Jackman: to administer the goods of her husband: cited by Strayne: ordered to accept or refuse the administration.

Thomas Tayler of Little Wilmcote and Elizabeth his wife: cited by Strayne: they did not appear: penalty reserved to the next court.

4 March 1624/5.

John Davis, shoemaker: 'for begettinge his wife with child before marriage': he appeared: admitted: ordered penance viz., 'to repayre to Mr. Baylife in the presence of him and Mr. Alderman, Mr. Trapp, in the churche of Stratford to acknowledge their fault betweene this day and Sunday come senight next'.

Elizabeth Wheler alias Davis his wife: similarly.

John Heminges alias Ames: to certify performance of penance: he appeared: ordered to acknowledge the fault before the congregation on Sunday week 'publickly in the church of Stratford in his usual apparrell from the beginning of sermon to the end of the same and

---

1   Matheus Baylies, fuller, buried 10 July 1623.

2   Edward Sandles and Vrsely Yeate, married 28 June 1623.

to certifie the court of his performance of the same' in the next court.

Page 68

The Lady Frekelton: citation by ways and means renewed.

Richard Bartlett: he stands excommunicated for non-appearance.

Edward Sandells and Ursula his wife: to certify performance of penance: Ursula appeared: ordered to perform penance before Sunday week on pain of excommunication.

John Barbar and Thomas Burnal, 'churchwardens of the hamlettes of Bishopton etc., for not providinge a surpluce': ordered to provide the same 'before the feast of Easter'.

George Byten: *no entry.*

Elizabeth Court: she stands excommunicated.

Page 69

VISITATION of Mr. Thomas Wilson, 3 May 1625.

STRATFORD

Sworn:-
William Smith, Richard Tiler, Henry Norman, Christopher Smith churchwardens.
Mr. Trapp, schoolmaster.
Mr. Simon Trapp, curate.
John Byers, Robert Jasons, John Barbar, Thomas Burnett, sidesmen.
Isaac Hitchcoxe, surgeon.
Edward Wilkes, surgeon.
John Bedam, schoolmaster to teach writing.

LUDDINGTON

William Smart, churchwarden.
William Mosely, sidesman. Fee received.

BISHOPTON

John Heminges, churchwarden.
John Adams, sidesman. Fee received.
John Davis and Elizabeth Davis alias Wheeler, his wife: to certify performance of penance.
John Heminges alias Ames: for the same: he appeared: ordered to perform penance in his usual attire on the next Sunday in the church of Stratford.

Edward Sandells and Ursula his wife: for the same: Ursula appeared: ordered to appear in the next court and to pay the fees on pain of excommunication.
Margin dismissed.

SELECT BOOK LIST

Arbuthnot, G. (Ed), *The Vestry Book of Stratford-upon-Avon* (1899).

Burgess, A., *Shakespeare* (1971).

Chambers, E.K., *William Shakespeare*, 2 vols. (1930).

Collinson, P., *The Elizabethan Puritan Movement* (1967).

de Groot, J.H., *The Shakespeares and the Old Faith* (1946).

Emmison, F.G., *Elizabethan Life: Morals and Customs* (in press)

Fox, L., *The Borough Town of Stratford-upon-Avon* (1964).

Fripp, E.I., *Master Richard Quiney* (1924); *Shakespeare's Stratford* (1928); *Shakespeare's Haunts near Stratford* (1929).

Fripp, E.I. (ed.; transcribed by R. Savage) *Minutes and Accounts of the Corporation of Stratford-upon-Avon*, Dugdale Society, vols. 1, 3, 5, 10 (1921-1930).

Halliday, F.E., *A Shakespeare Companion* (1952).

McGrath, P., *Puritans and Papists under Elizabeth I* (1967).

Marchant, R.A., *The Church under the Law . . . 1560-1640* (1969).

Raleigh, W. (ed.), *Shakespeare's England,* 2 vols. (1916, 1926).

Rowse, A.L., *The England of Elizabeth* (1950); *William Shakespeare* (1963).

Savage, R. (ed.), *The Parish Registers of Stratford-upon-Avon. Baptisms* (1897), *Marriages* (1898), *Burials* (1905), Parish Register Society.

Schoenbaum, S., *Shakespeare's Lives* (1971).

Styles, P., 'The Borough of Stratford-upon-Avon' in *The Victoria County History of the County of Warwick*, vol. 3 (1945).

Wilson, J. Dover, *Life in Shakespeare's England* (1949).

INDEX OF PERSONS

Note: *The various spellings of names are given, followed (in brackets) by offices, occupations etc. These are all of Stratford unless otherwise stated.*

c.w. = Churchwarden

INDEX OF PLACES

Note: *These are all in Warwickshire unless otherwise stated*